From Technical to Exceptional

From Technical to Exceptional: Transform to Outperform and Make Your Mark

Andrew Zeitoun

From Technical to Exceptional:
Transform to Outperform and Make Your Mark

ISBN-13: 978-1985603851
ISBN-10: 1985603853

Cover design by Luisito C. Pangilinan

Threshold Knowledge Inc.

www.tech2exceptional.com

Transitioning from a technical expert to a trusted business partner requires a different language set. This book covers that transformation in both language and thought process.

—Michael Cholubko

About the Author

Andrew Zeitoun has spent the last 20 years straddling the technology and management divide. He has filled many roles including technical pre-sales, system administration, IT Operations Management, as well as consulting and training. Even with such a diverse set of experiences, he finds himself always coming back to the consulting and training roles. Whether it's authoring or delivering technical and leadership courses, Andrew's passion is for helping people solve their own problems. Throughout his consulting work, Andrew saw that most of those problems were not technology problems, even though they had technical symptoms. With research conducted during his graduate studies, Andrew was able to bring many facets together, blending knowledge and practices.

Andrew founded Threshold Knowledge Inc. in 2004 with a focus on finding the practical balance between leadership and technology. Andrew actively leads consulting teams to support customers undertaking IT-led business critical projects in addition to coaching and training new and experienced managers.

Dedication

This book is dedicated to my wife, Kristi, and my children, Michael and Sarah. They were not only a constant source of encouragement, but also a constant source of fresh coffee that was critical for those long days and nights. Thank you for all your support!

This book is also dedicated to those people who helped me learn, grow and connect as I made my own transition from technical expert to something more. I am lucky to call some of you friends.

—Andrew

Table of Contents

List of Figures

List of Tables

Foreword

Like many technology professionals, my background in technology began well before I started thinking about a career. What started off as an interest and hobby evolved into a profession, and helping friends and family with their technology problems morphed into helping companies use technology to achieve their business objectives.

Early in my career, I was very focused on knowing everything about the technology we were working with. I always wanted to be the expert and worked hard to keep up to date on the latest networking solutions, management tools, and applications. Even as I moved up in seniority and began managing people and departments, I still held on to this feeling that I needed to be the expert so that, if my team needed me, I could jump in, guide them to the solution to a problem, or suggest a next best course of action.

I still remember when I realized that this was not the right strategy for me. I had been given accountability for some non-technical departments—business functions that I didn't have a direct background in. I quickly realized that I had no choice but to rely on my team to be the experts, and for me to focus on guiding the business, asking the right questions, and focusing on the customer. That was the point when I realized that I needed to take the same approach in the technical sphere as well. It was time for me to transform from technical to exceptional.

I attribute that fundamental shift in my approach with enabling my career path which led me from leading IT departments, to leading the entire back office and support group at a financial institution and then back into leading operations and technology for a technology business and ultimately into the CEO role.

As Andrew Zeitoun adeptly points out throughout this book, changing your approach—away from focusing on the technology and towards focusing on the business is critical to growing your influence and advancing your career. In my experience, the best place to start is with increasing the areas of your own curiosity. It is often easy to simply focus myopically on your own area of accountability and capability and to leave the rest to others. Avoid this temptation and force yourself to think about other dimensions of the business.

Be sure you know who the customers of the business are and always put yourself in their shoes, do not let anyone tell you that "your customers are other internal stakeholders". A business only has one customer and everyone from sales, marketing, IT, operations and finance must all be working together to meet their needs. Most importantly, have an opinion about everything that is happening in the company and don't be afraid to share it. Ask a lot of questions and find non-technical mentors that will help you broaden your approach.

Identify opportunities to participate in initiatives that are not limited to your technical areas of expertise. If there is a special project to look at a new product, volunteer. Raise your hand to sit on the job evaluation committee or the employee social committee. Offer to help a colleague who is working on something outside your comfort zone. Agree to represent the company at an industry event. Your objective should be to get exposed to as many parts of the company as possible and to build relationships in as many different areas as possible.

Once you have successfully shifted your own perspective and taken yourself to a place where you have a view as to the broader business, then you can truly begin to deliver value. Armed with this new found perspective and still equipped with your technology background and skills you can become the advocate for using technology to deliver customer value across the organization. You will find yourself being sought out as the person who can bridge the gap between the business and technology. You can now be the universal translator, helping your technology customers understand what the business people are asking for and helping the business people understand what the technologists are talking about.

I wish you the very best as you embark on your transformation journey.

—Andrew Obee, MBA
President & CEO, The Ficanex Group of Companies

Preface

Years ago, I found myself where many of you are today. I was a technical expert. I was deep into emerging technologies like Fibre Channel and fault-tolerant systems. I had written one of the first courses on high-performance storage network design to include Storage Area Network design. I was more interested in managing infrastructure than I was in solving pre-sales engineering puzzles. I got myself planted firmly in the back office.

My time in IT global operations gave me more opportunities to learn the hard way. Between leading projects and leading my team, there were learning opportunities everywhere I turned.
Eventually I returned to consulting and training. Half of my time was spent in purely technical training and the other half was spent in developing new managers and leaders. Those two streams ran parallel to one another for several years.

I started working on my graduate degree on the evolutionary nature of systems virtualization. By the time I had drafted my dissertation, most of the technological aspects had been brushed aside. The combination of research and observation finally brought my two parallel paths together. The first thing that struck me was that since the 1970s, the overall failure rate for technical projects has not improved despite all of the project methodologies that have been developed to address the problem. That says the issue is not about the project methodology. The realization was that over 80% of the problems weren't technical, they were people and communications problems with technical symptoms. While you as technical experts have the answers to the technical symptoms, you can't actually solve the problem without first fixing the people and communication problems.

I have made every mistake in this book, some of them twice, and I learned my lessons the hard way. My goal is to pass on as many of the things I've learned so it doesn't take you nearly as long to make your mark in your organization, your industry or your community.

This book focuses on project-based work, but the lessons and the transformation apply equally to project and process work.

This book may not take a project destined for failure and guarantee that you'll save it, there are too many variables outside of the scope of this book. There are common project killers: lack of high level executive sponsor who acts as a champion, insufficient budget or time available, lack of alignment within the senior levels of the organization, the list goes on. There are several good books that can help you identify those project threats. That's not the purpose here.

The goal of this book is to provide you with the knowledge and skills to take a project that meets the minimum criteria for success and helps you ensure that you deliver the right value and engage your stakeholder in the right way to make your project leadership exceptionally successful.

The benefits go far beyond the project you are managing right now. The transformations will change the way you interact with your stakeholders and will change the way that they view you.

Your reputation, your influence and your future can be exceptional with the knowledge you hold in your hands.

Acknowledgements

Many people have contributed to bringing this book to you. Their contributions made it more organized, coherent and usable. Any errors you may find, though, are mine alone.

First, a thank you to the other half of the Threshold Knowledge partnership, P.J. VanAuken. From the years of energy and effort spent refining our approach to leadership, management, organizational alignment to the painstaking review of every page in this book. I appreciate where you've flexed to support my work, where you've helped to keep me on track, and most important to me, where you've lead us to do the right things the right way.

A thank you goes out to Andre Noenchen, for being a sounding board for leadership ideas in an overly technical world over the years. I appreciate the work you did in reviewing this book and providing positive feedback.

Special thanks go to my first and oldest instructors, my parents. I was lucky enough, though I didn't see it that way at the time, to listen to project problems and technology tribulations as regular dinner table conversation. Some of what I know, I learned by osmosis long before I started my own career.

Thank you to John Estrella, who showed me how to take my thoughts and ideas and turn them in to a book faster than I believed was possible.

Finally, a heartfelt thank you to all my friends and colleagues, fellow authors and instructors, clients and students who have shared knowledge, asked questions or brought their problems to the table. Each of you has contributed in some way to the final work you see in front of you.

#TECH2EXCEPTIONAL #

INTRODUCTION

This book will be most valuable to you when you not only read the pages but think about the questions raised and answer them as they relate to your organization.

There are several tools built into the sections of the book that are designed to help you go beyond simply reading. They are provided to focus your thinking and help you answer the questions as they relate to your customers, your project and your organization.

Self-assessment: These help you establish a baseline and take your current knowledge, your current situation and use that information to point you in the direction of next steps tailored to where you are now.

Call to action: These are questions or steps in the analyses that you should do right there and then. Get the information before you try to go on. You will need that information to move foward in the book and you will need that information to be successful in your work.

Keys to success: Summarizing the main points in each chapter, they also serve as a good reminder after you've finished reading the book.

Pulling it all together: At the end of most chapters this section allows you to test yourself. Did you just read the chapter or did you do the work? If you can accurately answer the questions you will have gained the insight and knowledge you needed to make use of the transformational skills.

Remember: These sections appear throughout the chapters and focus your attention on a key point or take-away that may not be intuitive or easy to see at first.

As you progress through the book, if you find yourself challenged, lost or stuck, reach out. Send an email message to andrew@tech2exceptional.com or visit the website for ideas, resources and access to forums with people who have gone through these transformations and can tell you about their experiences. In addition, you'll find many of the analysis templates used in this book available for download.

List of Abbreviations

BA	Business Analyst
BSA	Business Systems Analyst
CEO	Chief Executive Officer
CFO	Chief Financial Officer
CIO	Chief Information Officer
COO	Chief Operating Officer
CTO	Chief Technical Officer
CM	Change Management
DoD	(US) Department of Defence
IM	Information Management
IS	Information System(s)
ISD	Information Systems Development
IT	Information Technology
ITRM	IT Relationship Management/Manager
KB	Knowledge Base
KBA	Knowledge Base Article
MD	Managing Director
MIS	Management Information Systems
OGC	Office of Government Commerce
OODA	Observe, Orient, Decide, Act
PgM	Program(me) Manager
PM	Project Manager
PMBOK®	Project Management Body of Knowledge
PRINCE2®	Projects in Controlled Environments
RM	Relationship Manager
SME	Subject Matter Expert
WS	Work System(s)
UAT	User Acceptance Testing
VP	Vice President

TRANSFORMATION 1

FROM DISILLUSIONED
TO EYES WIDE OPEN

As technical experts leading projects there are tremendous amounts of stress and pressure on you. It's hard enough to manage the technology pieces, but working with non-technical stakeholders can make it even harder. Sometimes it can feel like you are working on two different projects!

For a minute forget everything you know about running technical projects.

Your project success hinges more on how you interact and communicate with your non-technical stakeholders than the specifics of the technology you deliver. This bears repeating—it doesn't matter if you deliver the right technical solution if your business stakeholder doesn't believe it will work for them or worse, doesn't believe you built it to support their requirements.

Look at it another way: A good working relationship with your stakeholder can give you a second chance when technical implementations hit snags, but poor working relationships and low credibility can doom good working technology to the 'failed project' pile due to lack of adoption and lack of use by the user community.

To see how you're doing (or how you've done in the past) find a piece of paper and a pen (or an electronic equivalent) and answer the fifteen questions below. You can also do the self-assessment electronically. Go to www.tech2exceptional.com if pen and paper is not your thing.

Self-Assessment

Think of a past project that you worked on for a non-technical stakeholder.

Q1. What was your stakeholder's level of knowledge on what they wanted to accomplish at the beginning of the project?

A: Clear Vision   B: Some ideas   C: Vague

Q2. How satisfied was the stakeholder with the project deliverables?

A: Fully satisfied   B: Partially satisfied   C: Not satisfied

Q3. How easy was it to figure out what your stakeholder wanted to accomplish and how that fit into the technology requirements?

A: Easy   B: Some challenges   C: Difficult

Q4. How quickly/completely was the new system adopted/used?

A:Within a month   B: 3 to 12 months   C: Never adopted

Q5. How many project meetings were held with your stakeholder and their team trying to determine what to do or build?

A: None or more than 5 B: Three to Five   C:One or two

Q6. During meetings, how often do/did you think "Why do they keep going on about {some non-technical topic}? It's not important to getting this project under way!"

A: Never   B: Once   C: More than Once

Q7. Have you ever been frustrated because they won't listen to your expertise when you tell them something can't be done (or done a certain way)?

A: Never   B: Once   C: More than Once

Q8. How many times have you worked on a project where you delivered what the stakeholders asked for but then they complained about the new system?

A: Never   B: Once   C: More than Once

Q9. My stakeholder reads my email messages all the way through.

A: Yes   B: Sometimes   C: No

Q10. My stakeholder takes the time to listen to my explanations and recommendations

A: Yes   B: Sometimes   C: No

Q11. How often does your stakeholder interrupt your explanations?

A: Never   B: Once   C: More than Once

Q12. How often does your stakeholder push you for quick answers without thinking through the details?

A: Never   B: Once   C: More than Once

Q13. Were you able to get clear and usable answers from your stakeholder?

A: Yes   B: Sometimes   C: No

Q14. My project has _____ change requests once the detailed design phase has been completed

A: None   B: One or two   C: More than two

Q15. How much of the project needed to be reworked or changed before User Acceptance Testing UAT sign-off was achieved?

A: Less than 5%   B: 5% to 15%   C: More than 15%

Scoring Guide:

Add up all your As, Bs and Cs:

- A = 0 point
- B = 2 points
- C = 4 points

If your total score is between 0 and 12: You're almost there! You've managed to avoid many of the common pitfalls that catch technical project leaders unaware. Some of the transformational techniques will be familiar to you, and you'll get to perfect those. Some of the techniques will be new, or have a new angle to them; take the time to work through them and add them to your arsenal.

If your total score is between 13 and 29: On the right path. You may be instinctively doing some of the right things the right way, or you may be consciously working towards these transformations. Use this material to refine the ones you know and to start working on the new transformations.

If your total score is between 30 and 60: You are starting your journey. Most of the transformations covered here apply to you. Each one will challenge you in your comfort zone, and that will be hard for some people. The good news is you've already started.

Have you ever been on a project where you finally get to User Acceptance Testing (UAT) and out of the blue your stakeholder suddenly starts to question and object to things that they signed off on way back in the design phase?

They dig their heels in at User Acceptance Testing, if nowhere else, because suddenly it dawns on them that IT believes their part of the job is done and are about to step away. From the business perspective, the work isn't nearly done even though from an IT perspective you may think it is.

At the root of the problem we come down to the divide of 'us' and 'them'; IT and Business. It happens between other departments as well, but there is a greater divide between the technical and non-technical groups within an organization.

Technical experts are just that, experts at technology. By virtue of good results in technical matters, they are often allowed, asked, or assigned to lead projects. Sometimes the technologist will be armed with project management training, others go on without.

Some of the technical project managers have experience leading small groups or departments as team leads or managers. For others this is their first time integrating technical and non-technical project considerations. For other technical project managers, this will be the first time leading people and coordinating everything else.

---

*Your **stakeholders** are generally considered to be anyone that can have a significant impact on your ability to deliver a successful project.*

*Those who directly contribute to the delivery of what you are responsible for are **primary stakeholders**. This doesn't usually include your project contributors who are analysed in more depth under the heading of Project Team. Your primary stakeholder in this book is the person that you report to and who is responsible to the business for the delivery of this project. You can consider them your client.*

*Those who can indirectly influence the delivery of what you are responsible for are **secondary stakeholders**. They can either make it easier or harder to deliver project success.*

Despite your track record for success in the realm of technology, none of that makes for good interactions with non-technical stakeholders (Stakeholders from the non-technical business units in your organization). Even when the project management training and team leadership experience are in your favor, there are three key reasons that you struggle with your non-technical stakeholders: Business Knowledge, Credibility, and Communications.

By now you should be asking yourself "Why?", "Why should I care?" or "So how does this affect me?" If you're not there yet, that will come in the next chapter, but the answer is provided here as well.

Even if you don't want to leave your technical role, even if you don't want to be a manager, your track record with projects outside of IT has a profound impact on you and your career.

If you don't get this right, what is this costing you?

- Personal and professional credibility
- Time, energy, money (that you could be earning for the same effort)

- Job satisfaction
- It's costing you stress and preventing you from enjoying a part of your life

What can you do about it? You can adapt. You can transform. You can develop the skills and abilities and, most of all, the credibility to move out of the 'technician' bubble and act as a bridge to the business.

How can you take a different approach that works? How can you lead your projects more successfully?

If you want to get out of the hole you are in, you first need to know in what direction to go. Digging harder in the same direction you were going in before just means getting deeper in the hole.

Once you understand the forces and reactions that shape the patterns you see in your projects then you can find a way out. Put in other words, doing more of what got you into your existing situation won't get you out of that situation.

For many people, technical experts especially, Project Management certification is an intuitive way to start on the road to a career in Project Management. Unfortunately, on its own, all that does is make you more systematically focused, more process focused and less likely to succeed with your non-technical stakeholders because that's not the problem you have to solve.

To be successful as a technical project manager, you need to understand you are not set up for success and that the 'traditional' approaches to advancement aren't going to help. This isn't anything new, but the message is coming in to focus more day by day. As a technical subject matter expert, leading technical projects, you have three challenges to overcome: Value, Knowledge and Credibility. The goal is simple. Success. Your reputation, your advancement and, very likely, your sense of satisfaction are based on your track record for success.

Transformation Overview

The good news is that you've already started the transformation. You've taken the first step, the first of the Six Transformations. Each chapter will target one major transformation with the knowledge you need and the tools you can use to be successful. There is also a chapter for troubleshooting and making sure you are on track to succeed.

- Transformation 1: You Are Here
- Transformation 2: From Tech Savvy to Business Savvy
- Transformation 3: From Technical Resource to Strategic Partner
- Transformation 4: From Reluctantly Reclusive to Perfectly Persuasive
- Transformation 5: From Irritation to Interesting Interactions
- Transformation 6: From Super Stressed to Stunning Success
- Checkpoint and Troubleshooting

To be successful project managers, technologists need to understand:

- You are experiencing symptoms and not causes
- IT objectives are not Business objectives
- Business value is the key
- People listen when they trust your input
- People listen more when you speak their language
- How to get from 'good idea' to 'good result'
- Whatever technology you implement is not successful if it doesn't get used

Transformation in Motion

One of the symptoms that people, especially technical experts, overlook is the inner voice or gut feel. It's not logical, and on its own it may not tell you everything but developing the skill and ability to listen to your inner voice is important. That inner voice is often your first indicator that things are not right; that's a symptom. As you work through Transformation 4 you will see how refining that inner voice fits into your future success.

As you spend much of your day immersed in technology, it's easy to isolate yourself in your individual work. One of the first challenges that technical experts, including technical managers, run into is that Technology objectives are not Business objectives. This includes Information Systems (IS) or Information Technology (IT). For simplicity's sake, this book will generically refer to them as IT or Technology. In a perfect world, IT objectives would align with and support business objectives. Sometimes they drift, or the alignment isn't obvious to anyone outside your department.

A simple example is that IT usually has the ongoing responsibility for delivering cost-effective infrastructure and datacenter operations. IT often pursues objectives like standardization, consolidation and various technical innovations to achieve this. Marketing may have a departmental objective for revenue generation through a new Customer Relationship Management (CRM) system aligned with the organization's strategic plan.

If those two initiatives conflict, which has priority? Which should have priority?

Based on business Value, the marketing initiative, which is tied to the organization's strategy, should have priority over internal departmental initiatives.

---

*Time after time, one of the first questions that IT asks their stakeholders is **"Choose a server size and configuration from the IT Services Catalogue."** Any time a deviation is requested, the answer from IT is usually **"That's not a supported IT standard."***

This not only undermines potentially higher priority initiatives in the business but is an easy way to alienate your stakeholders. For more on this, see Transformation 3.

It's not that IT standards shouldn't exist. Departments should not be unilaterally able to force IT to support new, one-off platforms without higher level buy-in and increased funding. The point is that taking new business projects and shoe-horning them into existing IT standards before the requirements and the design are finalized is the first step on the road to project failure.

Depending on your organization, and your position in it, organizational objectives may take some translation before they are relevant to you. If you want to be successful, you'll spend the time to understand your organizational objectives from the top. In successful organizations, all objectives map back to Business Value.

Quantifying business value is not quick or easy. Some organizations use proxy metrics like Return on Investment and other Opportunity Cost capture tools. From a project management perspective, it can be helpful to know what, if anything, your organization does to determine business value. Whether your organization formally captures a business value metric, the key for you is that you understand the project-derived business value in basic qualitative terms.

For your purposes, there are two directions that you can take to achieve Business Value. The first is by giving your customer the ability to do something that is important to them that they could not do before. This is referred to as Customer Value. The other approach to generate Business Value is when you can deliver the same level of customer value but at a lower internal cost.

Regardless of what you think you know and what value you think you can add, unless you have personal credibility then your stakeholders are not likely to listen to you. You need to develop your leadership voice and your personal power before your stakeholders put much weight in what you say.

Organizational credibility is harder. As a technical project leader, you can develop your personal credibility but how the rest of your organization views IT will also impact how you are viewed. There are ways to work around this. Some of those approaches may make you feel like you're abandoning your technical persona, but that's not the case. What you will do is make it easier for your non-technical stakeholders to see value in the technical knowledge you have.

There are several ways to measure the success of a project, depending on who you ask, you'll get a different answer. The most basic answer is that in order for a project to be successful, the changes have to be implemented and adopted by the business and it has to deliver value to the organization.

Whatever change your project brings to the business, whether it's a new tool, process or capability not only needs to make it easier for the users to perform the work, but the users actually need to use it effectively. That's only half of a success. Unfortunately, this is where many organizational projects stop paying attention - at that half-way point. The rest gets passing lip service, if that. The other half is whether, as a technical project manager, your projects deliver something that makes your organization more successful. Business value is the key.

Where does the technology fit in all of this? In order to deliver business value, you need to understand what role the technology projects play in adding business value.

Technical experts *should* understand the role technology plays in adding business value. Project managers *must* understand it.

As a project manager you need to know this if you want to be successful; without this you lack credibility. Once you understand your organization's business realities, you're able to understand what kinds of things IT should be spending time and money on in order to support organizational objectives and generate business value. As you demonstrate that knowledge to your stakeholders, you gain credibility.

Once you have that credibility, then you can act as a partner in solving business problems. For some, this marks a shift from where IT is treated as order-takers and elevates you to a place from where you can help steer strategic implementation and direction. This directly equates to providing business value. It allows you to answer the question "What can the business enable our customers to do better now, and why does it matter? "

As your stakeholders and other key players reach the place where they have bought into your idea for change, where they trust you and buy into your plan, then you can lead a successful implementation.

Does this sound too easy? Some might think so. Others might find the concept foreign or terrifying. It's not easy, but it's not impossible either. Regardless of where you are in your journey as a project leader, the concepts and the tools you'll find in this book will help you find your road to success.

TRANSFORMATION

FROM TECH SAVVY
TO BUSINESS SAVVY

The transition from tech savvy to business savvy can be a challenge for many technical experts. Not because it's difficult at the beginning, but because people are often limited in their own mental silos. Even the distinction between "technical" and "business" is a reminder of that.

You will be successful in this transformation when:

- You can explain to your peers and your stakeholders how your business value is linked to your customer value
- Where you can demonstrate your ability to focus your project on where it delivers value to the business

In order to do that, you will need to be able to:

- Determine how your IT department adds business value outside of this project
- Understand how your stakeholder's department adds business value outside of this project
- Communicate how your project adds business value

As technologists, your focus is often on the technology specifics. That's what interests you, that's your area of specialization. This can present a problem because no one else really cares. Just like your eyes glaze over when the sales guy starts going on about his new customer engagement strategy, or the CFO starts droning on about quarterly revenue targets.

Unless you're in the business of selling technology, whether software, hardware or consulting services, the technology itself adds no customer value. Your technology department exists to support the rest of the business in delivering value to your customers.

Throughout the book, the term business is used generically to refer to multiple types of organizations: private sector, public sector, and not-for-profit. When analyzing customer value, the same principles are followed. The term business value is used instead of organizational value because it comes across more naturally in verbal communications. From here on in, business value and organizational value are used interchangeably.

The focus on value is the single most important aspect of this transformation, from a business perspective. Everything you do has to relate back to business value or you should not be doing it. Period.

Business derives value in two ways. The first one, and the one with the highest potential business impact, is by providing customer value. Customer value means that, through your product or service, you enable the customer to do something that's important to them, that they could not do before.

The other way to generate business value is by finding ways to do the things your business is doing now, but at a lower internal cost. This boils down to delivering the same goods and services more efficiently.

From a technologist's perspective, there should be one more category that covers Preventative maintenance, Disaster Recovery, Fail-over solutions. The work spent avoiding failures or disasters is a large part of what drives IT. IT security also falls into this category.

Your stakeholders don't care until you experience the failure or the downtime because it is suddenly real and tangible. From a business perspective, all of these are risk-avoidance or risk mitigation activities. The business sees them as insurance policies from an investment perspective.

What you need to do is tie it all back to customer value. Do your customers require 99.99% system availability so they can conduct their business? Are there government regulatory compliance issues that mandate data retention and recovery requirements? Keep the focus on how your technical proposal impacts business value.

Customer value is the root of business value. It is possible to improve on business value by optimizing the organization's ability to deliver a certain level of customer value. However, the first step is to actually deliver something that is of value to the customer. From that perspective, the focus on customer value is the single most important aspect of this transformation.

Project success also needs to be measured against business value. Even things like safety and compliance can be looked at through the lens of customer value. If your business can't operate because you were not compliant with government regulations, then you can't generate customer value.

Once you understand how your organization creates value for its customers, what strategies it pursues and how you provide value in that process, you will be Business Aware.

When you can steer what you do on the technology side to align with the desired business outcomes, you'll be business savvy.

Call to Action

You're not just going to read this chapter and be able to make progress without doing the work. As you read, you will need to either write down or go find out key pieces of information by asking the following questions.

- *What is your organization's vision?*
- *If you have a separate departmental vision, what is it?*
- *Who are your customers?*
- *What value does your business provide them?*
- *What is IT's reputation in the organization?*
- *What is the organization's opinion of IT?* (Ask or listen, don't guess!)

Who are Your Customers?

The first thing you need know is who your customers are.

It's a simple question, and simply put, the answer is that your customers are the people, the businesses and the organizations that pay you directly. They're not necessarily the ones that use your products or services. This is a critical distinction; your customers and your users are not necessarily the same groups.

It is normal to have multiple types of customer. Often customers with the same characteristics are grouped together for ease of analysis, especially if you have numerous small customers – for example, magazines publication or neighborhood grocery stores – individual and family consumers. With fewer large customers, you may want to treat them individually.

Regardless of the nature of your organization, your customers are the external parties that give you money directly for goods or services, willingly or not. These include:

- Goods and services purchasers
- Taxpayers
- Other government departments
- Donors
- Charitable organizations

There is no such thing as an 'internal' customer in this model.

Anyone who doesn't give you money is not a customer. They may, however, be your customer's customer. This makes them influencers but not customers. They may influence you through your customer, but you don't need to go through those iterations because when you focus on your direct customer's value, the descending levels of customer value get accounted for automatically because it relates back to your customer's value.

You do have to account for the other groups internal to your organization at this point. These are the groups and departments that either feed into the work you do or that take your work and further process it. They may be the groups that rely on your technology and services to support the work that they do. They're not customers, but they will be important to you in the next chapter.

It is worth repeating that the people who use your product are not your customers if someone else paid for it.

As an example: Imagine you're waiting in your doctor's office and there are current newspapers and magazines in the waiting room. You read one. Should the publisher of the periodical consider you a customer? No. That office or clinic that bought the subscription is the customer. You're the customer's customer. All your organization needs to focus on is its direct customers.

Once you are clear on who your customers are, you can look at customer value. For some groups of customers, determining what provides value is easy, for others it can be difficult.

Customer Value and Business Value

Delivering customer value means giving your customer something that allows them to do something that is important to them, that they could not do before. Sometimes this is a new capability, other times it is the ability to perform a function better, faster or cheaper, if that is important to them.

Rolling out the next version of your software package with a new color scheme and new fonts probably doesn't count as increasing customer value. Rolling out a new version of your software package with a new feature that helps your customer solve a problem more easily definitely provides customer value.

So how does customer value relate to business value?

Providing customer value is one of the ways to realize business value. Basically, by providing customers new capabilities that allow them to do things that are important to them, you generate business value. The other way to generate business value is by finding ways to do the things your business is doing now, but at a lower internal cost. This boils down to delivering the same goods and services more efficiently, or referred to more formally, reducing the Cost of Goods Sold (COGS), the Cost of Services or, more generically, Cost of Sales.

Once you have a list of your customers, you can analyse how your organization provides value to them.

Customer	The Customer Values	Our Product, Service or Capability

Table 1: Customer Value Data Gathering

By understanding what your customers value, your business can focus on innovating to deliver that value. In doing so, you generate business value.

The nature of your business will determine whether it's more important to effectively deliver new customer value or to improve the efficiency of what you currently deliver. Whether your organization is in the private sector, in the public sector,whether you're working with not-for-profits, the business of your business tells you three things:

• Who are your customers?
• What the nature of your competitive landscape looks like
• What strategies the business is going to use to bring value

If you're in the private sector, how your business is going to derive its competitive advantage is more flexible than in the public sector or in the not-for-profit world. That's simply because of the nature of your competition, your customers and the constraints by which you provide goods and services.

In the public sector, your customers are probably other governmental entities, unless you collect money directly from individuals and businesses.

The Business of Your Business

The "Business of your Business" refers to the nature of your business and that determines what kinds of general strategies your organization will pursue. There are several factors that you must consider including the nature of the competitive landscape and the nature of your customer groups. Understanding this is necessary for you to be able to speak in a language that your stakeholders understand and value. It demonstrates that you understand what their business is about and therefore your recommendations are going to be grounded in their reality.

In looking at the nature of the competitive landscape, the real world differs from academic models in several ways.

Jokes are meant to be funny, but often contain an important message. It's often said that people laugh at some jokes because they are funny, and some because they're true.

Here is a joke to remember for these analyses.

Q: What's the difference between theory and practice?
A: In theory, there is no difference.

Unlike in the textbooks, there are no purely competitive markets and there are few pure monopolies, even in areas like government services. In the real world, given enough time, your customers will find what they want or find ways to get it. That's important to your organization, because if you're not providing value to your customers, your customers will find it somewhere else.

Michael Porter has developed several models that can help you analyze the forces and characteristics of your organization and the environment that acts on it. The models feed into one another and together they help answer these questions:

- What does the environment around my organization look like?

41

- How does this affect the strategies my organization adopts to deliver value?
- How does my project or department deliver value when we do not directly deliver value to the customer?

To get those answers:

1. Use Porter's Five Forces model to get the answers you need for Porter's Generic Strategies.

2. Use those answers to determine what strategies will work best for your organization within Porter's Generic Strategies framework

3. Apply value chain analysis to determine where you add value when you are not directly interacting with the customer

Porter's Five Forces

Porter's Five Forces model is used to generate the information you need to determine your organization's recommended strategies.

While Porter's Five Forces model was originally designed to assess how competitive an industry was, it can be adapted to assess the impact of forces in public sector and not-for-profit environments as well.

When adapted, five forces are:

- Supplier Power
- Buyer Power
- Threat of New Entrants (Competitors)
- Threat of Substitutes
- Competitive Pressure

Supplier Power: Raw materials, components, labor, services and specialized knowledge

Suppliers can exert power when there are few suppliers, unique offerings or when the cost of switching suppliers is high. In these cases, suppliers can charge higher prices or refuse to work for your organization without additional concessions.

Buyer (Customer) Power: Buyer power is high when customers have alternative choices, and low when they have few easily available alternatives.

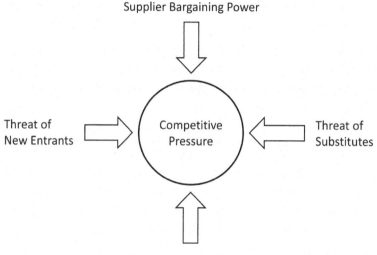

Figure 1: Porter's Five Forces Model (adapted)

Call to Action

Where does your organization rate on supplier power?

Where does your organization rate on buyer power?

Threat of Substitutes: Ease of substitution, availability of substitutes, buyer switching costs and perceived levels of differentiation.

The threat of substitutes needs to be considered closely in the public and the not-for-profit sectors. In the public sector this can appear as private sector offerings that eventually compete with public sector services. In some cases, they may manifest as privately supplied public service under the banners of: Privatization, Outsourcing and Alternate Service Delivery to name a few. There is very little in the public sector that is off limits. Whether you consider outsourcing of services like municipal waste collection or privatization of national postal services, the example scales all the way up to using private security contractor alongside or in place of standing militaries. Historically the term used was "mercenary".

In the not-for-profit sector, the threat of substitutes is most visible when you consider the pool of available donors at any point in time and the range of available charitable causes that they might support.

Threat of New Competitors: Economies of scale, brand loyalty, barriers to entry, perceived profitability of a market or industry.

From the perspective of understanding your organization's strategy, the threat of new competitors you most want to focus on is: Is there a customer need (value) that you are not fulfilling? That is most likely to align with your project and departmental objectives.

Call to Action

What is the threat of substitution to your organization?

What is the threat of new competitors?

Competitive Pressure: The combination of the previous four factors which tells you:

- How many direct competitors you have for a group of customers?
- How your customers perceive your product or service?
- How generic or differentiated it is from your competitors' products or services?
- How much flexibility and control your organization has over product or service pricing?
- How much impact or value is derived from pursuing Innovation strategies (increasing customer value) or optimization strategies (decreasing cost of delivering value)?

Competitive pressure directly affects the strategies your organization chooses

The answers to the five questions above are needed for Porter's Generic Strategies.

Porter's Generic Strategies

With the answers from Porter's Five Forces analysis, that information can be used to start building Porter's Generic Strategies model. This model has also been adapted to give insights applicable to private, public and not-for-profit sectors. The output of this model gives you an approximation of the types of strategies your organization will pursue in order to deliver business value.

Porter's generic strategies describe a 4-quadrant model that accounts for two major factors:

- How many competitors or potential substitutes exist for your product or service

- Whether your organization receives greater value from creating new customer value or reducing the cost of delivering existing customer value

Porter's generic strategies offers four approaches to delivering business value:

- **Cost Leadership:** Optimize the cost of goods or services so you can deliver them at market rates but achieve higher business value than competitors
- **Cost (Focus):** Segment your customer markets to create or target niches thereby reducing the number of competitors. Achieve cost leadership within those refined niches.
- **Differentiation:** Deliver new customer value by creating brand value and loyalty through the (customer) perceived differences in your product or service.
- **Differentiation (Focus):** Segment your customer markets to create or target niches thereby reducing the number of competitors. Differentiate your product or service and create brand value and loyalty.

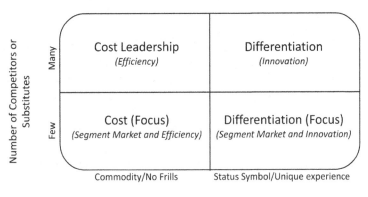

Figure 2: Porter's Generic Strategies Model (adapted)

For those in the public sector and the not-for-profit the same principle applies: How do you deliver enough customer value that your customers don't seek alternatives to meet their needs?

It allows you to answer questions like:

* How do you get more donors?
* How do you satisfy your donors more efficiently?
* How effectively do you deliver government services?
* How do you deliver governmental services more transparently and more evenly?
* How do you act as good custodians of taxpayer (or donor) money?

Though the wording is different at the root they're the same in terms of being able to consider the questions through Porter's Generic strategies

Private sector organizations may have more leeway in which strategies they use, while Public sector and not-for-profit focus on a moderate subset of the strategies. Value for the customer often includes feelings that the government is a good custodian of taxpayer's money. Customers also value the feeling that the government is making prudent choices with cost, value and transparency in mind.

Call to Action

Look at customer value, business value and generic strategies together. The project you're leading should be aligned with them. If it doesn't you need to figure out why.

If your project doesn't appear to align with the results of the Porter analysis, then a good first step is to figure out whether you have all the information you need. Most of the time you should be able to see the tie-in and alignment.

It's possible that your project is not aligned.

Your project could be tactical stop-gap, or it could be a fringe project. This means that your project could face disruption if another strategically aligned project needs your resources or funding because it will have a higher business value.

Being business savvy allows you to make those assessment and see those disruptions coming with more notice.

Porter's Value Chain

Unless you are in the business of selling technology, you are likely not delivering customer value directly, though you may be closer to the client through your work on a particular project.

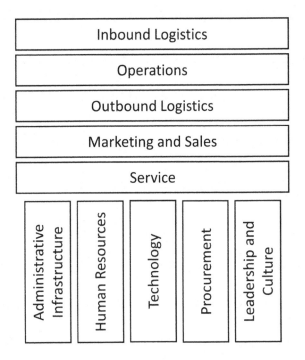

Figure 3: Porter's Value Chain (adapted)

Porter's Value Chain is a tool to help you understand and visualize how you contribute value that is eventually realized when it reaches the customer. It is a simple tool, but it can be powerful in helping you determine where and how value gets added internally in an organization.

The value chain model is a simple graphical representation of where in the organization your function sits and how what you do eventually becomes customer value add or business value add.

In the value chain model, there are two types of organizational activities: Primary and secondary (or supporting) activities. The five primary activities deliver value directly to the customer. The supporting activities encompass all the other activities that enhance, optimize and accelerate the primary activities.

It is important to understand the distinction because generating business value can happen in either Primary or Supporting Activities, by decreasing the cost of delivering value. Delivering increased customer value, by contrast, is only realized through innovation in the Primary activities.

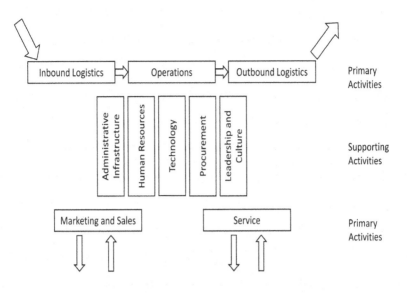

Figure 4: Expanded View of the Value Chain

You need to understand where you fit in to value chain and how your project and the technology add value to the business.

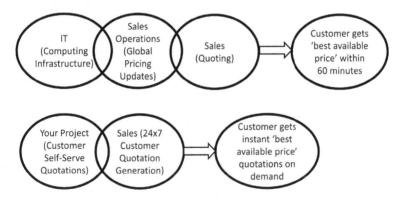

Figure 5: Value Chain Examples

The first value chain example shows the IT department in a typical back office role, providing the infrastructure that other business functions use to perform their daily work. IT works behind the scenes providing the computing infrastructure (desktops, laptops the tablets, the networks, all the technological connectivity) and it enables, in this example, Sales Operations to deliver global pricing updates. Sales Operations, the team responsible for global pricing update allows the Sales department, which is the customer facing function, to perform the quoting function that provides value to the customer. The overall value to the customer is that they get the pricing they want, for example, within 60 minutes of sending a quote request. IT, Sales Operations and Sales all contribute to the value chain in this example, but only through Sales is customer value delivered.

In the second example, there is a project that provides a customer self-service pricing portal. Here, a customer can login and generate their own quotes based on the price list without Sales having to be there to generate the quote. The customer gets the quotation on demand instantly, any time of any day, something that adds value for this category of customer.

One of the subtle differences between the two examples is when you improve the efficiency or effectiveness of IT in the first example, the benefits are wide-spread in the organization but do not create the same noticeable increase in customer value delivered. It represents a small efficiency gain across the organization at best. In many cases it doesn't even provide that, if there was no obvious inefficiency before the improvement.

In the second example, the effort and resources dedicated to deploying the customer self-service portal were more directed at creating distinctive customer value. It becomes easier to measure. It generally correlates to increase effectiveness rather than efficiency improvements.

In the first example, the organizational view tends towards efficiency activities, and when they are further away from the customer, are viewed from a cost-minimizing perspective. In the second example, the project activities are more likely to be viewed from a revenue-generating perspective.

It is easier to demonstrate the business value of revenue generating activities because they are more directly related to delivering customer value. There are also less intermediate steps and assumptions about efficiency that can be argued or disputed.

While it can be easier to be working on projects tied to revenue generation, there are ways to improve how you position organization efficiency projects. The key is to speak to the effect that those inefficiencies have on delivering customer value. For example, you should focus on the impact (of slow systems) on the customer, not on the sales person. These can be strengthened with research and data: "Studies show that our customers are willing to wait X minutes for a quote before looking at alternative suppliers and after Y minutes, they will choose another supplier even if our prices are lower."

Given a choice as a technologist, you want to have your role tied more closely to revenue generation and revenue recognition activities, assuming you have the credibility and you can demonstrate an understanding of the business. When you work on customer-facing or revenue-generating project, you generally have more leeway, you get more resources and, in some cases, less scrutiny than when you work in the back office. Items like infrastructure upgrades are often hard to get funding for unless something is actively breaking or slowing down or there is some other revenue generating function that justifies infrastructure expansion.

Project IOT and IAW

To go from business aware to business savvy means you need to be able to answer the "So what?" question – short for "So what does this mean to you?"

Answering "So what?" allows you to take the business knowledge and information and apply it to your project. This applies to all of your work.

Does what you're working in bring business value? How? If it doesn't generate business value, check again or ask yourself why bother doing it.

How does this knowledge influence the decisions you need to make?

The two tools to acronyms IAW and IOT work together to help you answer that question. IAW lives at the high level and it stands for "In Accordance With". That is "To deliver (your project) (and its goal or purpose)... in accordance with (a specific, defined organizational strategy)." The strategy question is answered when you can take your project and show how it aligns with the overall business or departmental strategy. IAW also helps define what parts of the strategy apply to you and your project.

IOT goes hand-in-hand with IAW and it stands for "In Order To". Where IAW answers the question "How does this project align?", IOT answers the question "Why are you doing this project?". The answer should tie back to the strategy either at the department or the organizational level and it should tell you what customer value looks like. It helps you understand the outcomes the project is looking for, and therefore the metrics that are important to measure. It tells you, in essence, how your organization is going to deliver business value.

Keys To Success

- When you focus on the technology before the business, you lose the focus on customer value
- If that happens, your stakeholders devalue your knowledge, your efforts and your technical experience because you don't

know what matters to them and the business. Or worse, it confirms what they already thought of you!

- When you get labelled that way, you automatically get limited in how much input you have – technically and otherwise. This will be covered more in the next chapter.
- When you focus on business value first, you show your stakeholders you understand the big picture and what success looks like to them. It may take time for them to listen to you, but this is how you start.

Pulling It All Together

Success in this transformation will come when you can fill out the following clearly and completely in order to use it to steer project decisions. The better your can articulate the points below, the more it demonstrates your business savvy and that's what this transformation is about.

The customer(s) that this project provides value to is/are:

_____

My project provides customer value because it allows them to do

_____ which is important

to them and they were unable to do before

OR

My project provides business value by reducing the cost of delivering products/services by

_____

TRANSFORMATION

FROM TECHNICAL RESOURCE
TO STRATEGIC PARTNER

When you're viewed as a technical resource by your organization that usually implies a few things, none of them are particularly good for your career or your ability to influence your organization. It tends to mean you're relegated to responsive or supporting roles, not leadership roles.

Stakeholders presume to know what you bring to the table.

They tell you what they want done, not provide you the big picture and ask for your recommendations. Make sure you ask about Business Value; remember IOT and IAW.

This happens less as your credibility improves.

In most private sector organizations, the further away you are from the customer translates to being further away from revenue-generating activities. This often leads to you getting boxed in by the organizational 'cost-center mentality'.

This can mean you don't get considered as part of building or growing the business and that equates to not being of primary importance.

You don't want to be viewed as a necessary cost to the organization. From a business perspective that means you're something to be tolerated and cost-minimized. It doesn't give you power or flexibility to deliver business value. You want to be a partner in these projects, a partner in organizational change. You want to be valued as a business asset who handles technology; a business asset who's good with technology but not limited by technology.

You want to be a business value enabler who uses technology!

As a final point, it's easy to outsource or replace technical resources. It's very hard to replace strategic partners.

The path to partnership:

- Build your business savvy (see Transformation 2)
- Build your personal credibility
- Build your power and influence
- Assess and avoid the risk of credibility drain based on your department's reputation

In order to become that strategic partner one of the first things you need to do is build your Personal Credibility. This builds directly on your Business Savvy from the previous transformation. With your credibility established, you need to build your influence and establish your personal power.

It's not a linear path because there are things outside of what you personally do that can impact your credibility and reputation, and so you'll need to take steps there to mitigate the risks.

Personal Credibility

How good you are with technology doesn't play into how competent you are viewed as being by the business. The reason for this is simple, most of the business stakeholders can't judge how competent you are in technology because they don't know that much about the technology. It's for this reason Business Savvy was covered before introducing personal credibility. Your stakeholders' perceptions, along with their biases and filters, have a material impact on your project and what you can accomplish. The goal is to understand and work around these challenges to accomplish what you want to.

The term 'Leadership Voice' is used to describe the messages that you convey and the way that you convey them. It includes the words you say, the way you say them, and the way people perceive them. It's about what you say you're going to do and what people see you doing. Your leadership voice is the impression that your audience forms from these various inputs, so your leadership voice is very important when it comes to leading projects, leading teams or simply trying to influence other people.

Call to Action

Avoid the technical jargon and acronyms. Speak the language of your business.

Your leadership voice affects everything you do in communications and a large part of your growing credibility is tied to strengthening your leadership voice. Strengthening your leadership voice is as much learning about yourself and how others perceive you as it is about learning new skills and techniques.

Knowing yourself and being authentic go hand-in-hand. They form the basis of developing your leadership voice. Authenticity is about behaving in a way that's true to you, not acting. Your team, your stakeholders, anyone you interact with will automatically look at the things you say and the things that you do for signs of alignment or misalignment. When the two don't align, you lose credibility and trust because people observe the difference between what you say and what you do. This observation and assessment often happen subconsciously. The people around you aren't consciously looking and comparing but it happens regardless and continually.

It's natural to wonder why others can't be more logical or rational in their decision making; to wonder why some people appear to make emotionally based decisions. That's a matter of perspective: most people believe they make rational and logical decisions, but the reality is far from that. People are not detached, clinical, and logical. They make emotionally based decisions that are influenced by their own experience, culture, and values which are then validated through logical justifications. Regardless of how logical you think you are, you are not immune to this.

"Be yourself" is not at odds with any of the transformations presented in the book. Being yourself means understanding your values, motivations and roles and operating in a way that is in line with them.

These transformations build on your understanding and knowledge of yourself. They allow you to flex your communication styles, reach out to stakeholders, consider the larger business and extend your influence and your power while staying true to yourself.

When it comes to credibility, "What you know", and "What you're known for" are two factors in your ability to influence and convince people.

Even when you make recommendations on technical decisions, your stakeholders will only accept your logical justification based on your credibility with that particular stakeholder. When your credibility is low, no amount of logical argument will sway your audience. Your stakeholders don't trust what you have to say.

Many technical experts, especially, get caught up in the trap of leading with logical arguments. To technical experts, they believe there is truth in the data or truth in the technology that is so apparent to them.

While it's true the data doesn't lie, all solutions are interpretations of the data presented. If your stakeholders don't trust you, that is if you don't have enough credibility with them, then no amount of data will get them to see your point of view. At the end of the day, the raw data doesn't have its own conclusions, conclusions are all interpretations. The question is whether your stakeholder trusts your interpretation.

Your credibility is going to start low with new people, with new stakeholders. Building your credibility takes time. How can you speed that up?

- Focus on what you've done in the past that relates to what you're doing now
- What's your track record for success?
- Leverage the portfolio of things that you've done
- Own your opinions, be upfront "I think ..." "Based on my experience..."
- Tie the objectives back to business and customer value, forget about the technology
- Call on the people who have had success in projects working with you

Demonstrate success where you've been successful. In those places that you failed, show that you have learned from failure. Be consistent and make use of your network. Think about who you know. Who knows both you and your stakeholder? Who could vouch for you, leveraging their credibility to improve your credibility? Remember the most important aspect of strengthening your credibility is by focusing your communication on what matters to your stakeholder.

Managers and Managers

As you work to build your credibility, you need to be aware of the potential credibility killers. One of those credibility killers that lurks subconsciously in most organizations is tied back to the very nature of the role of the project manager.

Most project managers are not line managers, that is, they don't have dedicated teams or departments. Project managers are assigned to one or more projects and their reports typically have dotted line relationships to the PM. The dotted line relationships to the Project Manager are in addition to a direct reporting relationship up to their respective line managers. While a dotted line relationship to the project manager as part of the project makes sense in theory, from a credibility perspective though it has negative impacts.

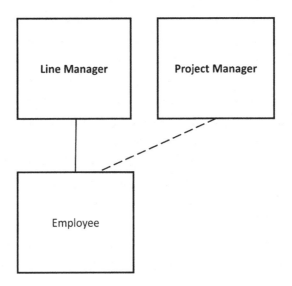

Figure 6: Team Member Reporting Relationships

Since project managers typically don't have direct reports, only the dotted line relationships, they are often not trained as line managers. From the organization's perspective PMs are not intended to be employed as line managers. Unfortunately, from a credibility perspective, this carries a cost.

From a credibility and authenticity perspective, the title Project Manager implies a management function – people management – and project managers who do not have direct reports or training in managing direct reports can lose credibility. Like many evaluations of your credibility and authenticity, this is done subconsciously by others. They evaluate your behavior, your actions and your choices measured through the lens of what they expect managers to do.

There's another truth, when you look at that organizational chart snippet. When a line manager and a project manager have conflicting needs for an employee's time, the solid line presents a visually stronger connection than the dotted line. Keep that in mind as you negotiate for the resources on your team up front and consider it as you get into critical times within your project. Your goal is to avoid, as much as possible, that conflict. If the conflict can't be avoided, then your goal is to achieve what the Business needs while maintaining your credibility. You can accomplish this by either being able to forego the use of a resource temporarily through your good project planning, or by getting the results you need even when your resource is being pulled in two directions.

There is one more area of complexity when it comes to reporting relationships and project managers.

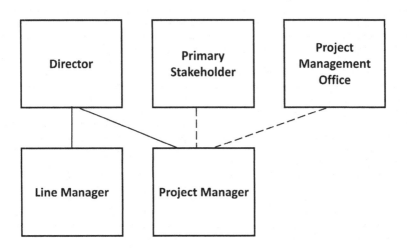

Figure 7: Project and Line Manager Reporting Relationships

As you reach the point of conducting stakeholder analysis in one of the upcoming transformations, remember that you not only have to deliver a successful project to your stakeholder but you still have a manager to whom you have a direct line reporting relationship as well.

At this point, you may want to put your hands up and say "But wait! I don't have training as a manager! I'm not supposed to be a manager that's not my job!" That's true, but the judgement remains because it's done subconsciously. No amount of logical justification by you or your organization changes this.

From a practical perspective there are two things you need to do if you don't have formal training or experience managing direct reports. The first is to understand some of what makes managers different, from contexts to roles and identify where those contexts and roles overlap naturally with Project Management in order to use those opportunities to model credible management behavior. The second thing you need to ensure you understand where you may run into scheduling and availability conflicts with the solid-line managers of your dotted-line resources.

Henry Mintzberg, a professor and management expert, described 10 different roles (Mintzberg, 1973) that a manager plays across three different sets of situations or contexts.

All of the manager roles start with the formal status and authority in being the manager. By virtue of the interpersonal roles, as the Figurehead, the Leader and the Liaison, the manager is further equipped to fulfil the informational roles.

Through the informational roles, as the Monitor, the Disseminator and the Spokesperson, the manager has the data and the context from which to make informed decisions. Those decisions are carried out through the Entrepreneur, the Disturbance Handler, the Resource Allocator and the Negotiator roles.

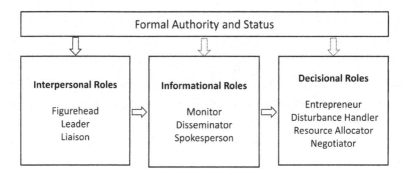

Figure 8: Mintzberg's Managerial Roles (adapted)

How do the Mintzberg management roles relate to your work as a project manager? Fortunately, they relate very well. You might argue that the entrepreneur role doesn't get fulfilled by the project manager once the project is in flight, however the remainder correlate one for one.

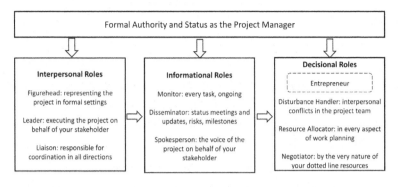

Figure 9: Mintzberg's Roles as a Project Manager

Influence and Personal Power

As you work on building your credibility, you're building your power.

It's important to note that there are two different kinds of power. Positional Authority is the kind of power that comes with the position and title of Project Manager (or Manager, Director, CEO, etc.) The second kind of power is known as Personal Power.

There is no 'good' or 'bad' power, each has its limitations. The key is to understand that and use the right tool for the job.

Power is the way you implement change. It is important that you know what power you have and how to use it effectively.

As a project manager you have Positional Authority which lets you start to get your job done. With enough Authority you can force through any of the changes you want by exercising that positional power, but there are consequences to this approach. You can make people do what you tell them, but you can't make them care, buy in, or put extra effort in. When you routinely rely on positional authority, you risk people giving you the bare minimum to comply with what you explicitly instructed them to do.

The strongest leaders, whether in business, families and social groups, are those who have Positional Authority but don't use it. They rely on their Personal Power instead.

There are three components to Personal Power:

- Information Power: Information you have or things you know
- Knowledge Power: What you know how to do
- Referent Power: The ability to influence those around you without use of direct authority

Building your personal power is an ongoing process. Many people are focused on Knowledge Power, often to the exclusion of Information and Referent Power. Efficient and effective growth in personal power requires the mix of all three.

For a project manager, building your information power starts with developing your Business Savvy. From there, it's about keeping your eyes and ears open. Read about your industry and others outside of your own. Understand what your organization is doing, what its strategies are. Your ability to keep up on technology won't do much for you here.

Knowledge power can start from where you excel at technology but needs to include other things. Your ability to organize and lead projects, negotiate for resources, juggle priorities, communicate and influence stakeholders, develop innovative solutions to business problems are examples of areas where you might develop your knowledge power.

Referent power is often misunderstood. In some cases, it is referred to as personal power (as a component of personal power). It is about a leader's ability to influence the people around them through interpersonal and relationship skills. Referent power is a function of people wanting to work with you and accomplish the vision you set out, not because they have to.

There are hundreds of articles and books written on developing your personal power. They approach the subject from all angles, from the psychological to the spiritual and religious. Many of the points have some simple, common threads. From your perspective as a technical project manager, this list has been adapted to present a professional focus:

- Find things that you are good at and develop your expertise
- Leverage that expertise as it relates to the project you are leading
- Develop a detailed vision of your project's success, the problem it will solve and the value it will bring
- Research and gather information about your project, your business, and the changes your project will bring about. Are your competitors doing it? Have some already done it? Are other fields and industries leading or following?
- Get excited about the problem you are solving or the value your project will deliver, don't be afraid to show it. This is your project, if you aren't excited and passionate about it, no one else will be either.
- Network inside and outside of your project. Focus on how your skills and knowledge can help others.
- Learn about yourself, your values and your motivations
- Be authentic in your words and your actions

Judged by the Company You Keep

Just like you must consider your reputation, how your organization views the IT department has a big impact on both you and your department's ability to lead change. How does your organization view IT?

- IT is always the problem: IT is something that the rest of the business has to protect against with restrictions, rules and regulations

- IT is an order taker: Fix this, deploy that. IT is expected to follow industry practices and support whatever strategic direction the business sets.
- IT is a strategic partner: a partner in leading organizational change

The answer matters because how your department is perceived shapes the business reaction to everything you do. It can be empowering if your departmental reputation is good and it can be limiting if the business considers you as less than an equal partner.

This has an impact on you as you build your credibility. If you have high credibility, but the department you belong to has lower credibility then your credibility will suffer in direct relationship to how closely aligned you are with your department.

This is a function of implicit and explicit attitude generalizations. There are three key aspects (Ranganath (Ratliff) & Nosek, 2008) related to attitude generalization:

- Some generalizations about members of a group are transferred to new group members immediately
- Other generalizations (explicit generalizations) can be resisted for a short period of time before being transferred to new members of a group. This is typically less than 24 hours.
- How strong or weak the effect of transferring these generalized traits is dependent on the perceived group entitativity. This refers to the extent which a collection of individuals is perceived as being a unified entity (Campbell, 1958).

When your department's reputation is strong, whether that reputation is good or bad, it will often trump what people think of you and your reputation as an individual. The more closely you are considered to be one of *'that'* department, the more your department's reputation will overshadow your own.

In terms of your project, your stakeholders, who evaluate your individual reputation, who interact with you on a daily basis, know that there are different people with different reputations in your department. As they work more regularly with you, they can keep the generalizations about your department separate from their assessment of your credibility. With new stakeholder or stakeholders that you do not interact with regularly (every few days as a minimum), your personal credibility will be affected by their generalized attitudes about your department.

When you are new to an organization, your credibility is even influenced by your predecessor, even if you've never even met them!

"If it looks like IT and it dresses like IT and it talks like IT then it must be IT."

This is a funny phrase but well known in the business side. If you identify closely with your IT department and your departmental reputation isn't better than yours then you're bringing your own reputation down by blending in with the crowd. Being easily identified as "an IT" person instead of having your own independent identity and credibility won't help you achieve your personal or project goals. This is referred to as high group entitativity.

You need to step out from under the shadow of your department.

Whether you change the way you dress is up to you, but from the previous transformation you certainly want to change:

- The things you talk about (Business focus not technology focus)

- The way you talk about them (Value added business solutions, not technical implementations) in the language that your stakeholder understands, not technical jargon

- Who you spend time with (do you always hang out with the IT crowd or do you have friends and contacts in other departments)? Do you make regular time to check in with your stakeholder and other business contributors?

These are the first steps to breaking away from the IT mould.

The second part is developing your identity with the project. Your project matters to your stakeholder and you want your stakeholder to know that the project outcomes matter to you too. Not just from a technology aspect, but from a business value perspective.

You want to make sure that your stakeholder understands that you share the same vision and the same project identity. The focus shouldn't be the differences; that you're from two different departments. Focus on the similarities; that you're working together on the project with the same vision and success criteria. That, in itself, will help you and your stakeholder work on developing a shared vocabulary.

Those three things: the shared Vision, shared Identity and shared Vocabulary are signs that you are doing the right things and that you're making the right Transformations, the right connections with your stakeholder.

Why does it matter? It matters because how your stakeholder feels about what you deliver on the project can have a bigger impact than what you actually deliver:

- If your stakeholder doesn't feel you're aligned and understand how to deliver the business outcomes, they are less likely to trust the decisions you've made related to the technical implementations

- You may have the right solution, but they don't believe in it (believe in you) and so their ability to get users to buy into using the system is low

- In early project delivery stages, it's normal to have drift between what the stakeholder envisions and what gets delivered in the prototype. When they have high confidence in you, it's easier for them to work with you to re-focus and refine the next attempt. If they have low confidence in you, it's easy for them to write you and the project off as failed or on the path to failure.

Keys To Success

You will be successful in this transformation when you develop the aspects of your leadership voice:

- your message
- how you deliver it
- how people hear it
- and how they feel about it

Your credibility and your personal power will directly affect your ability to influence your stakeholders and the degree that your team members want to work with you to achieve the shared vision. You'll be able to get things done for your project and success breeds success

Your track record of success will buy you more credibility with your stakeholders while stepping out from under the shadow of your department and cultivating your project-based identity will reinforce that.

You can't be just a nameless, faceless technologist if you want to succeed in this transformation and develop your reputation as an individual.

Pulling It All Together

Complete the following sentences to determine where you are in the tech savvy and business savvy continuum.

I am well known

☐ in my organization
☐ in my department
☐ in my team
☐ I'm not well known

I interact with people outside my department regularly through

☐ organizational sports teams
☐ social groups
☐ volunteering and community support organized through work
☐ I am intentional about regularly arranging lunch or coffee with people outside my department OR I'm a member of the smoker's club and accomplish my networking there
☐ nothing; I don't interact with people outside my department

During my breaks in the work day, I am usually

☐ socialising outside my department
☐ spending time with the people in my department
☐ working at my desk

As a project leader, who in your organization (outside of your own department) needs to know about you?

What kind of image or impression do they need to have of you if you are going to be successful?

What kinds of things can you do differently to achieve those results?

TRANSFORMATION 4

FROM RELUCTANTLY RECLUSIVE
TO PERFECTLY PERSUASIVE

Developing your leadership voice has two major areas of effort. The first area, understanding yourself, your motivations and values was covered in the previous Transformation. Packaged all together, it is the authentic you. The second major area is how you communicate your message effectively to your stakeholders.

In order to successfully communicate with your stakeholders, you need to be able to persuade them. You need to have the credibility, but more than that, you need to be able to communicate in a way that your stakeholder understands. You want to communicate in a way that they can relate to easily. You need to be able to transmit your message so that they can interpret it in the way you want them to:

- You will hold their attention longer
- They hear what you are trying to say
- They pay attention instead of answering other email messages
- Reduces the risk of misunderstanding.

To accomplish this, the process is broken down into two parts. The first part focuses how to identify the communication styles of your stakeholders. Once you know that, you can consider how you flex your communication style to adapt to your stakeholders. You want to be able to meet them where they're at, from a communications perspective. The reason for that is simple, you want specific outcomes from them, so you flex to accommodate, in order to achieve the results you want.

There is another area of capability that can help you improve your ability to deliver your message effectively to your stakeholder. It overlaps and intertwines with every aspect of your verbal communications. Emotional Intelligence (EI) is a term given to a cluster of related skills and everyone has Emotional Intelligence. The only question is to what degree you've developed yours.

For many, EI remains outside of the realm of conscious action. It will be a point of focus in order to bring it to the forefront. Improving your Emotional Intelligence will improve all of your stakeholder interactions. There is not enough room in this book to do more than introduce the fundamentals of EI and look at some of the indicators in your personal and professional life.

Stakeholder Communications

Have you ever worked with people and found it was instantly easy to communicate with them? Then you work with someone else and suddenly nothing you do seems to work in terms of communication understanding and misunderstandings.

A lot of that boils down to individual communication styles.

Everyone naturally has a style of communicating. When you communicate with somebody who's got a similar style to you, everything clicks because what comes out of your mouth naturally gets interpreted and aligns with their style. As a result, they find it very easy to follow along and understand what you're trying to convey. Since they have the same patterns in their communications and the same kinds of underlying thought processes, they are able to take what you say and make sense of it and respond back in a way that you understand easily.

With other stakeholders it's not so easy to communicate, especially when your stakeholders have very different communication styles to yours.

How can you identify someone's communication style?

There are some generalizations that help you approximate your stakeholder's communication style. These generalizations are just that, a starting point. Every individual is different, and you'll have to assess them based on your knowledge and interactions with them. People usually have a primary style and a secondary communication style. Even if you can only flex to one of them, your stakeholder will be able to effectively understand your message and the context in the way you want them to.

One of the models for identifying communications styles is based on the work of Dr. Eileen Russo. It has been simplified and adapted in the table below. The two dimensions of analysis are:

- Degree of stakeholder assertiveness
- Degree of stakeholder expressiveness

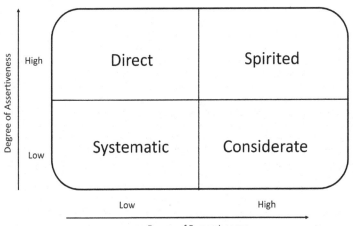

Figure 10: Communications Styles (adapted)

The communication styles analysis is based on observing a number of traits, based on the way they combine to form particular communications styles. There is an additional factor that can help you simplify your analysis. Various senior organizational roles tend to favor, or appeal to, people with particular communication tendencies, personalities and habits:

- Entrepreneurial stakeholders
  - o Typically responsible for new businesses, markets, products or innovation
  - o Tend to be very ideas focused
  - o High assertiveness, high expressiveness
  - o Tend to be classified as "spirited"

- IT or Finance stakeholders
  - o Tend towards analytical and detail oriented
  - o Typically favor time to assess and plan
  - o Low assertiveness, low expressiveness
  - o Tend to be classified as "systematic"

- CEOs and Presidents

o   Very focused on results and costs
o   Forceful in communications, little time for social interactions
o   High assertiveness, low expressiveness
o   Tend to be classified as "direct"

The Considerate Communication Style

Occasionally you will have stakeholders with their primary communication style as Considerate (high expressive, low assertive). It is more likely that you'll have them as members of your project team.

The Considerate communicator is focused on interpersonal relationships. That relationship and their ability to trust you are critical and allows the Considerate communicator to invest fully in your project. Simple things like saying "Good morning" or asking how they are doing can help develop that relationship **if** you ask genuinely and listen to the answer.

- Very focused on the welfare of others
- Hesitant to bring up points that may cause conflict or argument
- Often have pictures of, and talk about, their loved ones

The purpose of discussing generalized styles is to get you to start thinking about your stakeholders. You will need to understand your stakeholders and their preferred communications styles in detail.

The questions you need to have answers to include:

- How much detail your stakeholder wants to hear or see?
- How much supporting data they want before hearing your recommendation?
- How often do they want to be updated?
- At what level of decision making do they want to be consulted?

The answers you come up with will also change over time as your credibility increases with a particular stakeholder.

At a fundamental level, your stakeholders want to understand a few key things. Your goal is to deliver the answers in the way that is easiest for them to process with the lowest risk of misunderstanding.

- Can you achieve the desired outcome?
- How much will it cost?
- How long will it take?
- Preferred communications medium (face to face, telephone, email)?
- How often (daily status, milestones, only when problems are encountered)?

For technical experts, one of the hardest challenges is in flexing your communication style. The tendency towards detail oriented, systematic and process focused can make it difficult to deliver the message you need to in a way that your stakeholders can process easily.

If your stakeholder is Direct

The first skill you need is the ability to talk the top line. What is the end result? What is the summary? This is important in both written (email) and verbal communications with your direct stakeholder.

A simple rule of thumb, as most of these stakeholders will read their messages on a mobile device, is that the top line must fit on one screen. If your stakeholder needs to scroll, then you've lost their attention. Whether your stakeholder is conscious of it or not, you have made yourself a lower priority in their day because if they have to stop what they are currently working on to read and digest your email message, they will put it aside until later (and later may never happen). On the other hand, if you make it easy for them to give you the answers you need, and they can continue their busy day, you've made yourself easy to prioritize up.

Some militaries use the acronym BLUF to reinforce the discipline of delivering those messages. It stands for Bottom Line Up Front. Don't write in the order you think. Don't write like you're building an academic article. You still must do your preparatory work, the data gathering, analysis, recommendation proposal. You then put that all aside and you draft a very short, concise message.

To: Bob the stakeholder
Subject: Action Required: Choosing a supplier

Bob,

If we do not successfully choose a supplier today and notify them before the end of business, the project will miss its deadline.

Recommendation,
I recommend we work with Sally's technology group to...

Rationale:

All the analysis, research and stuff that went into the recommendation. No one is going to read this, but you'll feel better at least knowing they have the option.

Figure 11: Direct Stakeholder Communication Example

The idea of sending a message that short and direct is unnerving to some people. It could easily be shorter, assuming you have a high enough level of credibility with your stakeholder. Keep in mind that while that note may feel short and direct to you, most Direct and

Spirited stakeholders confess frustration with technologists need to live in the minutiae.

BLUF takes practice, especially if the approach is new to you.

If you struggle with the process, or if you are starting with low credibility, you can include some of the factors that went into your recommendation or decision later in the email message. That's critical. There can be no extraneous text in the critical window where you need your stakeholder's attention and action.

There are a few areas to watch out for with your Direct stakeholder. By being aware of these areas of concern, you can understand them for what they are, just a direct communicator in action.

- Can be a poor listener, especially if you're going too slowly or are not talking about what they are interested in
- Is impatient with others (see above)
- Does not heed advice
- Likes to argue
- Competitive
- Discounts feelings
- Overlooks details

This doesn't make this stakeholder a bad person or bad at their job, on the contrary being a Direct communicator makes them a great fit for certain roles. If you can understand what communication traps to avoid and flex your communication to their style you will have someone on your side who is driven to push your project through.

There are top six ways to flex your style to your Direct stakeholder.

1. Focus on their goals and objectives
2. Keep your relationship businesslike
3. Argue facts, not feelings or beliefs
4. Be well organized in your presentation
5. Ask questions directly

6. Speak at a fast pace, but not rushed

If your stakeholder is Spirited

Spirited stakeholders are high energy, love to be the center of attention and have great ideas. In fact, their sense of self is directly tied to their ideas.

So, the first skill you need to develop to deal with your Spirited stakeholder is your ability to hold your tongue. They will have crazy ideas that you know right off won't work. Don't shoot them down. A Spirited communicator will take your unwillingness to consider their idea as a personal attack. Instead, hear them out. Understand what they are trying to accomplish. Get excited about their end goal. Then, ask permission to help put together a plan to get there. This way, you can still address all the risks that jumped to mind the minute they opened their mouth.

Allow a Spirited stakeholder to be part of the brainstorming process. When it comes time to explore the details, they will likely excuse themselves as this is not an area of interest or talent for them, in fact they will often generalize or gloss over important details. Don't expect them to dig into those details, this is an area that you can take over or find someone else on the team to do.

Spirited stakeholders are high energy, you need to match that energy level. Spirited communicators respond best to face to face or phone conversations so limit the use of email as much as possible. Ideally, just use it to summarize the action items of your face to face meeting.

To: Bob the stakeholder
Subject: Thanks! Great Meeting!

Hi Bob,
Thanks for a great meeting today, I'm excited to be working on this project with you.
Coming out of the meeting we agreed that:

- I'd update the project plan with the new dates

- I'll set up the next working session for brainstorming

- You will prepare and facilitate the brainstorming discussion

Let me know if you have anything else to add!

Figure 12: Spirited Stakeholder Communication Example

As with the Direct communicator, there are a couple of areas of concern to watch out for with a Spirited Communicator.

- Tend to not hear details
- Tends to exaggerate
- Generalizes
- Can be overly dramatic
- Responds poorly to criticism
- Glosses over details – over simplifies
- Tends to miss deadlines
- Does not manage time efficiently

Again, if you focus on the positive aspects of this style, they can energize a room and a project. However, being aware of the trouble spots will help you achieve success.

Top six ways to flex your style to your Spirited stakeholder:

1. Focus on inspiring ideas, visions of success
2. Be supportive of their ideas, there is a difference between supporting the idea and agreeing with the steps to get there
3. Don't hurry the discussion
4. Engage in brainstorming. Instead of "but what if?" try for "do you know what else this would do for us?"
5. Be entertaining and fast moving
6. Allow them to share their ideas freely in a supportive environment

If your stakeholder is Systematic

Systematic stakeholders may be easiest for many technical people to work with as chances are good that they share the same or similar styles.

Systematic communicators thrive on information so the first skill you need to develop when talking to a Systematic stakeholder is research. The more information they have, the more confident they feel in their decision. Ensure that you have done your homework before approaching a systematic person with a plan. They will be looking for that missing detail and then will likely hyper fixate on that point and may miss the overall objective. Avoid going to them with ideas, wait until you have a plan. They will dismiss your idea, not because it doesn't have merit, but because you clearly haven't put enough research time into it.

Once you have a plan spend some time thinking about the questions you will be asked and prepare those answers as well. A failure to answer their questions will be a sign of a plan that hasn't been well thought out.

Finally, build time in your plan for your Systematic stakeholder to do their own analysis and get back to you with questions, feedback or alignment to your plan. This type of communicator will be very challenged to give you an immediate answer. Don't misunderstand, this is not a reflection on your credibility with them, they will want to do their own analysis with almost any plan.

Written communication tends to be the method of choice for Systematic people. It avoids the interpersonal communication and awkwardness, has built in processing time and provides them all the details they require in a concrete way.

There is a strong possibility that you won't be able to keep your communications short enough to fit on one smartphone screen with a Systematic stakeholder and still be able to provide the level of precision and depth they will want. That doesn't generate the same problems as with a Direct stakeholder. Remember to make use of attachments where possible so that your supporting data can be laid out clearly and logically.

To: Bob the stakeholder

(4) Attachments

Subject: Project analysis update #3

Bob,

I've re-visited the research (see attached) and have identified gaps in the risk management plan.

I recommend the following 3 steps. I've also attached my detailed analysis so you can see where the recommendations came from and what the alternatives are:

- Review the current out-source contracts to understand the impact of losing a key contracted developer

- Determine whether we have internal resources with some of the key skill sets (attached list)

- Update the risk management plan and project timelines

We need to provide an answer to Sally by the end of the week, so if you could give me your feedback by Friday morning I'd appreciate it.

Figure 13: Systematic Stakeholder Communication Example

As with all communication styles, there are a couple of areas of concern to be aware of with a Systematic Communicator.

- Focus too much on details, to the exclusion of the big picture
- Fears personal disclosure
- Can be terse
- Uses little variety in vocal tones
- Puts accuracy ahead of feelings
- Tends to be impersonal
- Does not take risks
- Delays decision making
- May not see the need to focus on communicating a compelling vision

If you focus on the positive aspects of this style, your project will be well thought out and all risks accounted for.

Top six ways to flex your style to your Systematic stakeholder:

1. Focus on facts, not opinions
2. Be thorough and organized. Demonstrate that you've thought it through thoroughly.
3. Provide data when possible. How it's presented and organized will be scrutinized.
4. Be precise in your presentations. Precise words, phrases, terminology.
5. Avoid verbal gimmicks (exaggeration, hyperbole, metaphor)
6. Allow your stakeholder time for their own analysis

If your stakeholder is Considerate

Considerate stakeholders thrive on relationships and harmony. They take care of the wellbeing of the people around them.

The first skill you need to develop when dealing with a Considerate stakeholder is to slow down and be thoughtful. Bring them a coffee (or whatever they drink) to the start of your meeting with them. Ask them how they are doing, ask about their family, and learn about their interests. Really listen to the answers they give you and remember the details they shared (write it down after the meeting if you need to). Try sharing something about yourself too. While it may appear to be wasting precious time, this ice breaking time will energize your Considerate stakeholder and get them to a point where they want to work with you.

Considerate stakeholders will be very concerned about upsetting you or being too critical so they may be slow to provide constructive feedback. Be very intentional about asking them for their input as they won't necessarily provide it without an explicit invitation. When they provide challenges to your plan, listen without getting upset. If you react strongly or defensively, a Considerate stakeholder will retreat and not provide feedback in the future. Thank them for their feedback and express how it will help to make the project even more successful.

Considerate stakeholders need to feel valued, not just for the work they produce but for who they are. Take time to say thank you.

The Considerate communicator is not immune to communication challenges.

- Avoids conflict
- Give in rather than trigger conflict
- Trust is developed by demonstrating care for your Considerate stakeholder
- Overemphasizes feelings (yours, theirs)
- Prefers what is comfortable
- Allows own needs to linger, sometimes causing problems downstream
- Resists change
- Tells others what they want to hear

To: Bob the stakeholder

Subject: Good morning!

Hi Bob - How did your ball game go last night? Did you guys win?

By way of an update, the project you helped me with last month was a huge success. I couldn't have done it without you, so thank you!

I was thinking about the problem we discussed yesterday and feel that the right course of action is to bring it to the wider team.

What do you think? I'll be in my office this afternoon if you want to pop by for a chat.

Thanks again,

Figure 14: Considerate Stakeholder Communication Example

Focusing on the positive aspects of this style will ensure your team is taken care of and that interpersonal needs are met. A Considerate stakeholder will be supportive and works well in a team environment. However, be aware that Considerate stakeholders are easily hurt and will disengage if that happens.

Top six ways to flex your style to your Considerate stakeholder:

1. Focus on your relationship (Say good morning, ask how they are doing and care about the answer)

2. Consider and be supportive of their feelings (Raising your voice for emphasis will get them to shut down)
3. Make sure you understand their needs (They won't tell you unless they trust you and you ask them)
4. Be informal
5. Maintain a relaxed pace (avoiding conflict and stress)
6. Give them time to build trust in you and show them that you can be trusted

Achieving End Outcomes

Another area where technical experts tend to get stuck is when your stakeholder presses you for immediate answers. If you've spent your professional life developing accurate, analytical answers, this can be jarring, but it will be a common problem for you. There are a few things you can do to make it easier.

The first one is to anticipate the questions. Your Direct, and to a lesser extent your Spirited stakeholders, will be looking for fast answers. If you understand the logic behind the flow of the questions, you may find it easier to prepare your answers:

- Can you achieve the desired outcome? Yes or No. If the answer is no, your stakeholder doesn't care about the details
- How long will it take?
- How much will it cost?
- What is the business going to get out of it?

If you are not sure what kind of answers your stakeholder is looking for, there are several ways you can approach this. For example:

"I can't give you a fast answer with 100% certainty. Do you want an answer right now, or can I have ___ hours to give you a firm recommendation?"

Or,

"Based on the information I have right now, I'd say ___, however, if I can have ___ hours, I can give you something with a higher degree of certainty."

Most of the time your stakeholders are looking to answer a question in their own mind: Should the business proceed with this project?

Until your stakeholder gets the information they need, they will not be interested in any of the details you might have to provide. With that understanding, your next tool is the ability to estimate and the willingness to give an imprecise answer based on incomplete data. Often it can be beneficial to turn the questions around in order to conduct your quick analysis:

What will the business get out of this?	• The project will provide a system that delivers business value by (delivering increased customer value/decreasing the cost to deliver customer value) • If this project is designed to solve a problem, say so • The provide will (provide/improve) capabilities for (project user teams) by allowing them to _____
How long will this take?	• How many technical skill-sets do you need? Developers, administrators, operations? • Count the major phases: Requirements, design, deploy, test, migrate, validate and user training • For each phase: What is your low estimate? What is your high estimate? Average them out.
How much will this cost?	• Unless you know what the costs are up front, you may want to defer this question

	• If you have an IT Service Catalogue, you can estimate some of the costs quickly
Can we achieve the desired outcome?	• This should be a qualified yes.... • What business processes are going to be impacted? Which users? Who needs to buy in or sign off? • Your qualified yes should be based on having those critical preconditions for success

Table 2: Framework for High-Level Answers

Your stakeholders have limited time and limited attention and as much as they want to spend time with your project because it's important to them, they don't have that time to give. There are a few things you need to remember: The Devil is the Details. The details are not important to your stakeholders. Your job is to be competent and capable in order to manage the details. You stakeholders expect that you will look at the data, review the information, conduct the analysis and stand behind a recommendation. Unless you have very low credibility with them, they're not going to want to review the data but if you ask them to, or open up the option for them to review it, they may see it as a lack of confidence on your part and you may lose credibility with them.

Remember

Your job is to analyze the detail, summarize your recommendations and present them to your stakeholder in a way that makes it easy for them to trust you.

Sometimes, however, you will need details that you don't have. One of the questions you should ask your stakeholder is who on their team should you ask for particular detailed information. You're not going to ask about technology – your job is to recommend the technology. You will be asking about business requirements, customer requirements, current processes, current pain points and the like.

In many ways the world of IT and Technology is like its own language. Native speakers assume everyone else understands that language. For example, in North America if you speak English, you assume that everyone will be able to understand you, it is a fair and safe assumption. However, if you go to the Netherlands and speak only English, you will find that some people understand you and some don't. Suddenly your assumption that everyone speaks your language carries risk. The further away you get away from major cities and metropolitan areas, the less chance there is of being understood. So, imagine your CEO speaks Dutch and your entrepreneurs speak French, when you speak to them in English some words and phrases may carry over and other certainly don't. So, just like it is not wise to walk into a small town in northern France without the ability to speak a little French, you need to be able to flex to the language of your stakeholders.

Sometimes words and phrases not only don't translate well, but have the opposite effect of what you want. These phrases can kill off the discussion or get them to go in a direction you don't want to go. For example, if a Spirited stakeholder presents an idea and you respond with "that won't work" or "no", the conversation is over. You may think you are helping by mitigating risk and helping them think through their plan better. However, that Spirited person is now done talking to you, you've just stomped on what is most important to them. Remember, a better way would be to share in the excitement and validate their idea. Letting them know you can see what they are trying to achieve and asking permission to make a couple suggestions to make it even better. Now they see you as part of the team and will engage in brainstorming with you. You get the same end outcome and the risk is mitigated, but you did it without shutting down the conversation and most importantly, the relationship.

For technologists, the idea of backup systems and redundancy is a good thing. It means that you have a way to handle failures and you have ways to handle unplanned outages. However, when translated to the language of a financier or from an entrepreneurial perspective, these are bad words. It means you spent money on something that is going to sit around and do nothing.

The key to positioning these types of expenditures and initiatives involves understanding your stakeholder and understanding the language that they speak. You need to understand what's important to them. Instead of talking about "what if" scenarios, talk about growth scenarios. "It will allow us to handle new business requirements" or "it ensures we are ready to handle the high level of customer orders resulting from this year's marketing plan". If your stakeholder is motivated by financial and fiscal responsibility, talk about that. "Spending on this now will save us $x in the long run". Whichever way you choose to rephrase requires you to first think about your stakeholder and what matters to them and then to repackage what you want to accomplish in a way that speaks to their motivators.

Emotional Intelligence Applied

Emotional intelligence is a term originally given to a cluster of skills by Daniel Goleman and those skills directly correlate with how successful you will be at interacting with others. High emotional intelligence, measured as Emotional Quotient (EQ), equals High degree of success in communicating with others. High communication success leads to higher stakeholder satisfaction and higher communication success leads to better project implementations. Communicating with Emotional Intelligence gives you a significant advantage.

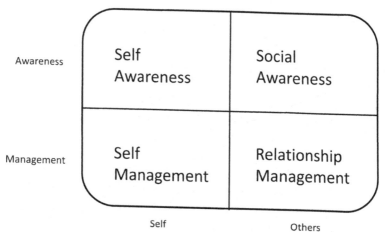

Figure 15: Four Quadrants of Emotional Intelligence

Observing Emotional Intelligence in action, you will see the four areas of focus:

- Self-awareness answers questions like: How are you feeling about the conversation? How are you feeling about the topic of conversation? How are you feeling about the person with whom you're having the conversation? Self-awareness is about your feelings and sensations in the moment.

- Self-management allows you to consciously choose a response to a situation in a deliberate way instead of impulsively.

- Social awareness allows you to read your audience. Are they interested? Are you about to lose them? Are they tracking? Do they understand?

- Relationship management allows you to take the input from the other three (self-awareness, self-management, and social awareness) and adapt your communication to reach your stakeholder more effectively.

One of the ways to improve your EQ is to practice, starting with self-awareness. Think about the answers honestly, your goal is to improve, not justify what you are doing today. If you're in doubt about your own biases and blind spots, think about how your colleagues at work or your boss might answer these questions about you. **Do not go and ask them directly!**

Self Awareness

- Do you find yourself experiencing sudden strong emotions?
- Do you find yourself reacting more strongly to a situation than those around you?
- Do you only use the words: happy, sad, angry, disgusted, fearful, surprised to describe how you feel?

Self Management

- Do you ever say things to people that you later regret?
- Do you say or do things that, while they may make you feel better, don't improve a situation?

Social Awareness

- Do you have trouble telling when someone has understood your point or your presentation?
- Do you find yourself saying the wrong things or bringing up topics at the wrong time?
- Would others describe you as insensitive?

Relationship Management

- Do you value the emotions of other people and the roles they play in the workplace?
- Do you know how to use your emotions and the emotions of others to get the best from your team?

Another aspect to self-awareness was touched on in the first Transformation. One of the ways to improve is to spend time observing your own emotions and your own reactions in different situations. Your gut feelings often let you know that something is out of place or not-quite-right.

Gut feelings are frequently ignored because they're not logical.

Logic, though, has almost nothing to do with this. There is nothing strictly logical about people because so much of the individual programming is done at the subconscious level that is impossible for an outside observer to know and anticipate; things like culture.

You would need to have full knowledge of other people, more than what you consciously know about yourself, to be able to understand the personal logic that people use. Without having full knowledge of themselves, people can be best described as making emotional decisions with logical justifications.

With high enough self-awareness and correspondingly high social awareness you can start to read people as they operate emotionally.

You can even work on your EI skills when you're on your own. Watch new or unfamiliar movies with the volume muted and no subtitles so you don't get to see or hear the dialogue. See how well you can follow the plot and the interactions. See if you can guess the feelings and emotions that are conveyed (obviously lip reading doesn't count).

To speed up your EI skill development, there are books and courses designed to hone your skills. In-person courses can be the fastest way to get you started and to improve your skills dramatically.

Keys To Success

Step1: Understand your stakeholder

- What is their communication style?
- How much do they want to know and how much do they want you to consult them on?
- Who can they refer you to for detailed questions on process and procedure?

Your stakeholder isn't your go-to for details.

Sometimes what you need is somebody from your stakeholder's team that understands more of the detailed business or procedural aspects. Your stakeholder may not have that data readily available, but you can always ask that they point you to the right person on their team that can answer the more detailed questions.

Step 2: Use their time wisely

- You typically have one bullet point to get your Stakeholder's attention; choose it wisely
- Your stakeholder won't listen to what you think is important until you've answered what they think is important

Step 3: Your job is to transform the data and make recommendations, not present the data:

- Review the project objectives and vision
- Review the data
- Come up with a recommendation and stand behind it
- Don't give them all the information and wait for your stakeholder to make a decision; that's not their job, that's yours (a Systematic stakeholder might want to do their own analysis but that doesn't get you off the hook for doing yours)

- When you update your stakeholder, how much do they want to know, how frequently do they want updates?
- Understand their preferred medium for communications and their preferred frequency
- Keep your updates short; if you can't fit it into 1 smartphone screen's worth then you haven't summarized it well enough (except with the Systematic stakeholder)

Step 4: Communicate and act with Emotional Intelligence:

- Be aware of what you're bringing to the table (credibility, communication style, reputation)
- Be aware of how you're reacting and the impact it may have on others
- Tailor your message and your delivery to achieve the aim you want

Pulling It All Together

Even if your credibility with your stakeholder is low, you need to ask your stakeholder business related questions in order to understand the bigger picture and make recommendations in line with that.

Even with low credibility, you can ask the question related to scope 'Are you going to run this report again? Is this going to be used for other customers?' Your stakeholder may not listen to you the first time, but if you're right it will help you develop the credibility that causes your stakeholders to listen to you more closely in the future.

TRANSFORMATION 5

FROM IRRITATION
TO INTERESTING INTERACTIONS

In the previous Transformation, one of the aims was to tailor your communications to best reach your stakeholders.

This transformation shifts your focus to how you manage your projects: how you run them and your mindset as it relates to key decision points.

To be successful in this Transformation you need to understand your project success criteria and its relation to business value in order to be able to adapt as business conditions change.

As a technologist coming into the project management role, the ability to initiate and nurture relationships is an outcome of being able to apply your business savvy and communicate effectively with your stakeholders.

With your business savvy and your technical savvy, you will be able to merge your knowledge of business outcomes, project objectives and your knowledge of IT services and processes. It is this combination that will allow you to explore and promote innovative solutions paving the way for project success and stakeholder satisfaction.

A taste of success

The concept of 'success' is not universal, nor is it objective. It is highly subjective, context-specific and usually has a number of implied conditions that are never made explicit. This is the root of many problems.

Remember

The issue of implicit requirements isn't always malicious. In many ways this is 'cultural' programming in action. This programming makes it easy for homogenous groups to communicate rapidly and it makes it easy for heterogenous groups to fail spectacularly.

Chasing the essence of success can be even harder for technical subject matter experts; you are often focused on all of the things you know, and that you need to get right, so that you don't have the energy to focus on what success is. Your focus should be on what success means to the people whose perspective matters most. When you don't have access to customer feedback directly, your next best option is your stakeholder's feedback as a proxy for your customers.

People and organizations continue to struggle with the definition of success, especially as it relates to projects. There are two major views of success: those that are easy to define and those that are easy to measure. The two have very little overlap in the real world.

In this Transformation it is not critical to be able to precisely measure business value attributed to your project. It is sufficient to be able to describe successful outcomes qualitatively if not quantitatively. The purpose here isn't to justify or defend your project, it is to continue the understanding of how your project is linked to specified business outcomes.

Success is context specific. This is one of the reasons that the concept of shared vision is so important. Without that shared vision different project members could have different interpretations of success.

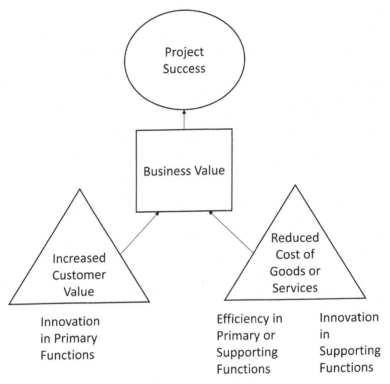

Figure 16: A Model of Project Success

What does success look like? For a programmer it might look like delivering code that compiles and runs. For a technician, it may be installing and configuring new software. This example can be extended to as many technical aspects as you like. These are the technical world-views that are important pre-conditions for success but not success by themselves.

The subject of what success looks like has been covered in many research papers. Three of the intersecting models are highlighted below. They are the Delone and McLean model of IS Success (Delone & McLean, Information Systems Success: The Quest for the Dependent Variable, 1992), Seddon's Conceptualized Model of IS Success (Seddon & al, 1999) and Alter's improved model (Delone & McLean, 2002). These models of success highlight three key points.

The first point is that organizational (business) value is only achieved when the technology, as part of a work system, gets used by the users providing them with individual value.

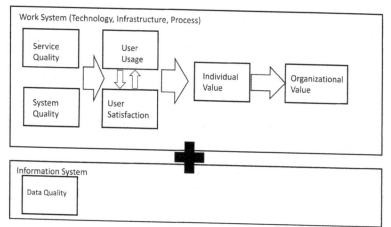

Figure 17: Composite Model of Success

The second point, highlighted by the Alter model, is that the evaluation of the project systems' effectiveness is a subjective evaluation made by your stakeholder.

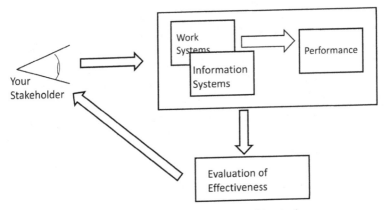

Figure 18: Success is Measured Subjectively

The third point, adapted from Seddon's Conceptualized Model of IS Success is that system use only happens as a result of the users' positive expectations about the benefits of using the new system.

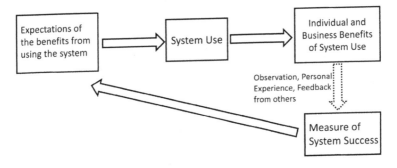

Figure 19: Feedback Cycle in System Adoption

By taking these points together and working backwards from the desired end-state the following deductions can be made:

- The combination of the technical systems, the processes and the quality of data available feeds into both how the users use the system and their satisfaction in doing so. The weakest link determines how happy your users will be, and how much they will use the system.

- Your stakeholder makes subjective assessments of the effectiveness of the project based on observation of the system in use and the feedback from the users. This determines whether your stakeholder thinks you delivered a successful project.

- The users need to understand the benefits (your project vision) before they have any motivation to use your systems. The more they buy into the vision of that positive change, they more motivated they will be to use the system. When communicating to the users, highlight the parts that are specifically relevant to them and the positive impacts the project will have on them.

In some cases, you'll be working on a project where the project outcomes and project success don't seem to align with business success or add business value. If that's the case the first step is to sit down with your stakeholder and ask for information. Ask for insight into how the project aligns with business value and the organization's strategic intent. You may get information that helps you see the connection.

Focus on the end-state. What will this project achieve, do or provide, not on the route to get there.

On rare occasion, you may find out that the project you're working on isn't strategic. Maybe it's a tactical stop-gap. In any case these are the answers you need to have before you move the project forward.

Projects Change

Most of the time changes to a project, once in flight, are considered negative or something to be avoided. You are constantly told to avoid scope creep. You put a lot of effort into building project charters, managing change logs and enforcing the need for project change requests. There are unintended outcomes of using these tools prescriptively, the main one being that project changes are deferred or ignored for the sake of meeting delivery deadlines and budgets.

Steven Covey often commented on the difference between Efficiency and Effectiveness.

"If the ladder is not leaning against the right wall, every step we take just gets us to the wrong place faster."

—*Stephen Covey*

Project managers have a number of tools at their disposal to ensure project efficiency, but you have to know when to use the tools, and when not to. There is no benefit to delivering an ineffective project efficiently.

Sometimes changing business requirements impact projects in flight, and as a project manager you need to understand when those are important, when those are relevant, and when those changes are what's right for the business. It may take more time, it may take more money, and it will certainly take more effort from you to adapt to that change, but that leads you back to the question of what success looks like to your organization. If you're not measuring against business success, what are you measuring against?

As business needs change over time, you need to be able to accept and adapt to changing project requirements. This is not an excuse to throw away good project management techniques in requirements management, scope control, and clarity of vision. When new information comes up that affects the business value proposition of a project, the stakeholder and your project need to adapt.

Your stakeholder (and their superiors) will usually be responsible for determining the business value of changing the project scope and requirements. Your role is to determine, or at least provide input on, the cost of those changes. This covers all aspects of project cost and resourcing including impacts to the project timeline.

Your objective is not to stop legitimate project changes. Your goal is to make sure your stakeholder has accurate information, so they can compare costs and benefits.

Understand why a project changes, as that impacts how you respond.

- Did the vision change?
- Did the value proposition change?
- Did someone get new information?

In an organizational environment that fosters project success, you should not be coerced to change a project's scope in flight without the additional time and resources you require. It would be naïve to believe that is the case universally. Death March, by Edward Yourdon, paints a bleak picture of what happens organizationally and personally when the organizational culture is built on pushing project managers to unrealistic goals and deadlines. While that can achieve the check in the box for project completion, it often fails to deliver real customer or business value.

If you and your stakeholder ignore the analysis steps and push on to finish a project as originally scoped and promised, you risk turning a useful project into a useless one. The project could become a waste of the time and resources because it does not achieve the business value it otherwise should have.

How can you adapt to changing business requirements? Sometimes it's easiest to start from first principles. Mnemonics like OODA can be used to describe the decision cycle and highlight the steps you need to take.

OODA: OBSERVE, ORIENT, DECIDE, ACT

The OODA Loop is a model developed by US Air Force Colonel John Boyd to describe the decision-making process. Originally used to describe the process of decision-making in combat, the OODA loop is commonly used to analyse and improve the responsiveness of both individual and organizational decision making.

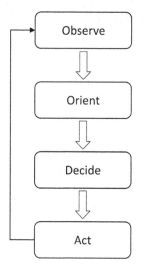

Observe
- New information, new business requirements or changing assumptions are brought to the project team's attention

Orient
- Review original project objectives and business value projections
- Review project assumptions
- Analyse new business information
- Identify other potential solutions for achieving business value at reduced project risk

Decide
- Based on the projected difference in business value, the projected difference in project costs and timeline assess the costs and benefits of the project change
- Does this change the project vision?

Act
- Keys stakeholders and executive sponsors must commit to the decision
- The project documentation must be changed
- Vision reformulated
- New project direction must be communicated widely and repeatedly

Figure 20: The OODA Loop

One of the dangers that comes with changing project directions is that your Supporters, their users, and your Resistors will not get the change, understand the change or follow the change in direction. It certainly won't happen quickly. You can expect to have to communicate the changed vision ten times more vigorously than you communicated the original one. That in itself carries a cost and introduces risk that you need to account for.

The Myth of the IT Project

One of the challenges technologist face is the concept of a technology or an IT project. Outside of the realm of pure theoretically research, there is no such thing as a technology project. They don't exist.

The reason is simple: If the technical work doesn't have an impact on the business, making no changes to user capability or functionality, then it may be a complex and costly set of procedures, but it is not a project. It becomes an expensive way to maintain the status quo.

Most of what gets passed off as a technology or an IT project is really a business transformation project that has a technology component. There's a big difference. A business transformation project is something that changes the way the users in your business operate.

It helps to think about it from the people and process side rather than the technology side. Will the users have to do different things than they do now? Would they have to do the normal things differently? Does it change their workflow? Does it change their procedures? If you answered yes to any of the last four questions, you're changing an aspect of the business by implementing technology. To some degree or another, that makes your project a business transformation project.

Knowing that you are leading a business transformation project should trigger the obvious question: Why is IT leading this? As the projects become higher profile, and higher risk, it becomes more important to ask that question.

The risks are important because you need plan for them and mitigate them based on your assessment of the situation. When you try to force users to change their workflow, process or tools through an IT led project, you will often experience significant push-back. In reviewing the 3 different models of systems success, you'll see how that can be the difference between project success and failure from your stakeholder's point of view.

The danger of an IT led business transformation executed as an IT project is that the technology becomes the focal point for user push-back. Whether the technology is difficult to learn, slower to use, less reliable, or any number of other excuses, it doesn't matter. With enough user complaint, the best you'll achieve is a system that users are slow to adopt or use as little as possible. That will not help you realize business value. In the worst case, the user pushback will result in your project being stalled, terminated or re-scoped, wasting time and money.

If users can push back against the technology tools enough, they can often stop the organizational change from happening. Often the excuses that are used to prevent the change are just that – excuses.

In contrast, when the project is run correctly as a business transformation, then there is usually time allocated to handling the process of user engagement, requirements, and acceptance testing. In addition, the process change component typically happens before or along side the proposed technology changes. If there is significant push back on the technology, another technology can be substituted without losing significant ground in the process change piece. In short, users cannot derail the organizational change because of complaints about the tool. The organizational change will happen, possibly with a different tool.

If IT is ill-suited to lead business transformation projects, why is IT leading this project? There are several reasons:

- Sometimes it's habit or organizational culture: IT has project managers and project managers lead projects...
- Sometimes the project crosses so many departmental boundaries and the infrastructure and technology are the only common components across the spectrum giving IT a unique insight into all of the needs of the participating departments
- IT (hardware and software) often consume the bulk of the project budget
- The final reason is that sometimes technology is intimidating to non-technologist so in order to get the technology part right, technologist get assigned to lead the project

Improving Your Odds

Some organizations have had such poor experience with technologist leading projects that they've added new layers between the business and technology. One such position is the IT Relationship Manager (ITRM). Introducing ITRMs to run projects adds several layers of complexity.

To improve the quality of your results in general project environments, you don't need to become an IT Relationship Manager, you just need to make use of the skills and the techniques that ITRMs use. You want to use the knowledge that the ITRMs have in order to improve your project management results.

So where does IT Relationship Management shine? There are four key areas:

- The ability to initiate and nurture relationships
- An understanding of the business environment and its needs
- Knowledge of IT services and processes
- The ability to explore and promote innovative solutions

The order of these is important: relationships are first, the business knowledge comes second, IT is third and when you have those in the right order then, you can look at innovative solutions.

When it comes to the risks associated with business transformation projects in the guise of IT projects, there are additional ways you can mitigate the risk to the project and to your credibility:

- Work with your primary stakeholder to develop a clear vision for the project end-state
- Identify the people and processes impacted
- Identify the decision makers, people managers and process owners these will effectively be additional stakeholders for you
- Determine which of these additional stakeholders are likely to be Supporters or Resistors of your project
- Conduct stakeholder analysis on your Supporters and Resistors
- Work with your primary stakeholder, sharing your analysis and develop joint plans for mitigating risk and converting Resistors to Supporters
- Make sure you have built enough time and resources to be able to tackle the fundamental business transformation aspects (covered further in the next Transformation)

Outside of your project team, you have four types of additional stakeholder that you need to consider. The two dimensions of analysis are: How much influence do they have? And how do they feel towards you and your project? This information can be charted easily in a four-quadrant diagram.

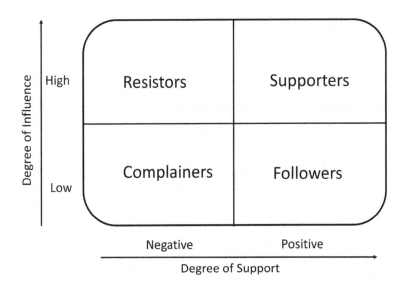

Figure 21: Charting Supporters and Resistors

Stakeholder analysis can be time consuming, so it is limited to your high-impact stakeholders, both Resistors and Supporters, if time permits. If not, start with your Resistors. The goal of the analysis is to get enough information and insight into your additional stakeholders that you can understand their priorities and motivations in order to tailor your communications effectively to them.

The Three P's of Stakeholder Analysis: Priorities, Perspectives and Personalities

This model starts from the superficial – that is the things that are easy to imagine or consider and then gets to the things that live in the semiconscious and subconscious. You can deduce their existence through the actions and behaviors of your stakeholder, but you can't identify them directly. Incidentally, these are the things that are hardest to see in yourself as well.

Priorities: Typically the easiest data to gather.

- What is important to accomplish? To deliver?
- What do they want to avoid/minimize?
- Where do they spend their time? With whom and on what?
- What do they have on their whiteboard? What have they sent in email?
- What tasks do their people talk about or focus on?
- What is their department, position, and role?
- What is someone in this role expected to do/deliver in the organization?

Perspectives: Partially conscious, partially subconscious; harder to determine.

- What words do they use?
- What are their hot buttons?
- What are their motivators?
- The perspectives of a Vice President of Sales will be very different from the Director of Customer Service and different again from the Chief Financial Officer

Personality: Most challenging, operating primarily at the subconscious level.

- Communication style
- Are they more leaders (focused on effectiveness and change)?
- Are they more managers (focused on optimizing current processes and deliverables)?
- Their culture, educational experiences, work history

You may not have enough knowledge of these Resistors and Supporters to generate all 3 P's. If you can't fill some of these out, think about them. Think about the indicators. Do some research; ask your Supporters and Followers. Think about the role they hold in the organization – what are the driving characteristics?

What are they expected to deliver (whether you agree with any of these or not)? What are their incentives based on? What kinds of decisions have they made in the past that you did not agree with? Assuming they are rational and skilled, what factors might have led them to choose that? What light does this shed on their 3P?

Don't forget to use your network. Use your primary stakeholder and their network as well. The more you know about your Resistors, the better chance you have to deliver the right messages to turn them into Supporters. Analysing your Supporters, on the other hand, is important because you want to know why your Supporters are supporting you. What's in it for them? What's important to them? (So you know to continue delivering those messages)

As you look at expanding the number of stakeholders you have to deal with, don't lose track of a critical truth: your ability to influence your stakeholders is at its peak when you work one-on-one with them. Group meetings are a bad place to introduce new material and a bad place to get buy-in and support. You may have to hold group meetings, but that doesn't prevent you from having one-on-one meetings before the meeting. Use those opportunities to:

- Listen to that stakeholder with no other distractions
- Target your messaging to what matters most to them in the communication style that resonates with them
- Adjust based on your level of credibility with that stakeholder
- Refine and repeat the vision of your project end-state and how it addresses their individual pain points or priorities

Keys To Success

Project success is defined:

- Project success = increased business value
- Business value = increased customer value or decreased cost of delivering goods or services
- Increased customer value = Innovation (delivering a new or improved capability that fulfills a customer need)
- Decreased cost of delivering goods or services = Efficiency (delivering an existing level of customer value at a reduced cost to the organization)

Project success is measured:

- The combination of the technical systems, the processes and the quality of data available feeds into both how the users use the system and their satisfaction in doing so. The weakest link determines how happy your users will be, and how much they will use the system.
- Your stakeholder makes subjective assessments of the effectiveness of the project based on observation of the system in use and the feedback from the users. This determines whether your stakeholder thinks you delivered a successful project.
- The users need to understand the benefits (your project vision) before they have any motivation to use your systems. The more they buy into the vision of that positive change, they more motivated they will be to use the system.

Pulling It All Together

My additional stakeholders are:

_____

_____

Supporters:

_____

_____

Resistors:

_____

_____

Resistor: _____	Supporter: _____
Priorities:	Priorities:
Perspectives:	Perspectives:
Personality:	Personality:

Figure 22: Stakeholder Analysis Template

TRANSFORMATION

FROM SUPER STRESSED
TO STUNNING SUCCESS

The final transformation focuses on delivering project success. This does not replace your PMI or PRINCE2 methodologies but puts context around them and steers you in the interpersonal space.

To be successful in this transformation, you need to understand how IT and Business alignment is the natural extension of focusing on customer and business value. This alignment is either strengthened or weakened at every level, including your project.

When dealing with business transformation projects, large and small, you need to be familiar with the critical preconditions to successful change initiatives.

Finally, you will need to be able to assess your project and make a judgement call on whether, for the sake of project and business success, you need to engage additional stakeholders in to leadership and supporting roles.

IT and Business Alignment

In organizations where there are high levels of IT/Business alignment, the risks associated with business transformations triggered by technology implementation are reduced. This is because IT/Business alignment means that IT initiated actions or projects are done with a degree of business awareness and organizational coordination, effectively reducing the areas where IT may work at cross purposes to the business.

The essence of alignment is how IT and the Business work together on a goal that brings value to the customer. Transformation number two started down this path. This Transformation finishes it.

Historically, alignment has been considered at the organizational strategic level. This is important, but alignment neither begins nor ends there. A good Chief Information Officer (CIO) or Chief Technology Officer (CTO) can establish the bridge that jump starts an alignment process, but the work must be carried down through the IT managers and established, tested and proven every day at the project manager and operational support levels.

Without continually delivered success, the CIO's credibility and the business's goodwill will evaporate. IT/Business alignment is either strengthened daily or it weakens daily. There is no neutral ground as every day brings new tasks, challenges, projects and goals. Each of those can cause misalignment between the business and IT

Remember

There is a direct link between alignment and your credibility.

IT Alignment improves with trust and a track record of delivering successful projects and tasks. This leads to positive outcomes including developing a common vocabulary between IT and the business and shared domain knowledge (Reich & Benbasat, 2000). This combination of common vocabulary and shared domain knowledge leads to IT knowledgeable line managers and business knowledgeable IT managers (Subrami & al, 1999). The key indicator of alignment is shared domain knowledge between business and IT. This can be viewed as the degree of overlap between the mutual knowledge of capabilities between Business and IT. When shared domain knowledge is high, communications between the two groups is frequent and effective, resulting in a high level of alignment.

What kinds of things destroy alignment at the project level?

- A focus on what you have, do or know before the stakeholder feels you know and care about their concerns
- Define IT-centric solutions before your stakeholder feels that project requirements have been specified to their satisfaction
- Fail to deliver on promised tasks
- Present the stakeholder with technical data and details instead of summarizing and recommending solutions
- When you focus on the details of the steps you're going to take, not what it will deliver or accomplish
- Limit communications frequency and style to suit yourself instead of your stakeholder

What happens when alignment is low?

- Relationship issues between Business and IT have been shown (Hatzakis & al, 2005) to lead to inefficiency and ineffectiveness in Information Systems development projects
- Poor project outcomes lead to relationship and trust issues between Business and IT (Lucas, 1975)
- In order to break out of this downward cycle, you as a project manager need to improve communications between the Business and IT, specifically between your project stakeholders and yourself

- This must happen before, during, and after technical projects in order to improve relationships between Business and IT colleagues and to ensure delivery of successful project results (Hatzakis & al, 2005)

When there is a lack of shared domain knowledge, the lack of common vocabulary and lack of shared identity contribute to breakdowns between IT and the business. The symptoms appear as differences in perceptions, goals, and interests, and they manifest as conflicts in your interactions and communications breakdowns.

The focus of the Six Transformations is to set the stage for improved IT/Business alignment by changing the knowledge, behavior and attitudes of the technical experts leading projects to focus first on business value instead of technological details.

Remembering that the way you project your leadership voice is apparent to your audience, but not as apparent to you without introspective practice, your attitudes and behaviors are easily interpreted by the business stakeholders. There is a measurable effect on the people you have to deal with and by changing these, you can better engage your business stakeholders leading to improved project outcomes.

Eight Deadly Sins in Change Leadership

John Kotter, Professor of Leadership Emeritus at the Harvard Business School, has written several books on organizational change leadership. In his writings, he identifies the eight preconditions to successful organization change projects. The structure and the knowledge of the eight steps are very helpful to smaller projects but critical to larger organizational change initiatives. These are summarized in his book "Leading Change" (Kotter, 1996).

Precondition 1: Generate a sense of urgency

If this is missing: Lack of urgency allows organizational leaders to avoid difficult decisions and steps by deferring indefinitely. Without the sense of urgency, the answer to the question "What happens if we don't change anything?" is nothing.

The sense of urgency has to exist at the highest level of project sponsorship, but that alone is not enough. You and your primary stakeholder have to be able to instill a sense of urgency in the other stakeholders: the Supporters and Resistors. Once you've created that sense of urgency, you need to maintain it throughout the project to get the ongoing support and attention from your stakeholders. Project started doesn't mean problem solved!

Call to Action

What happens if the change your project is supposed to bring about doesn't go through? What is the impact on Customer Value?

What are your stakeholders' pain points and motivators from your Stakeholder (3P) analysis?

Ensure your stakeholder analysis includes the stakeholders from both categories (Resistors and Supporters)

You need to connect to fears and motivations of your stakeholders to the sense of urgency. Logical arguments will not generate the urgency you need.

Remember

To connect with your Stakeholder's motivations, lead with your credibility or focus on the urgency of the situation. Use logic to support your points, not to lead the conversation.

Precondition 2: Build a powerful guiding coalition

If this is missing: Trying to carry a complex change initiative with too few Supporters means that no matter how motivated and capable they are, they will be worn down, circumvented or out-waited by active Resistors and passive employees who are change averse.

Your project needs to be able to fight the countervailing forces of Resistors, as well as those who are change averse. This is not a job for 1, 2 or 5 people. It may take 10, 20, or even 50 people depending on the nature of the change. Too few people will get tired and can get over-run.

The senior executive you have as a project sponsor needs to be more than that. They need to be an active champion to the project. That on its own is not enough. Your guiding coalition has to include your executive sponsor plus the divisional or line managers who are affected by the changes. Once you have the Supporters, you need to be able to articulate what you need from them. Any easy way to remember is 3H, or Head, Heart, Hands. Head is what you need your stakeholders to know or understand. Heart is how you want them to feel. Hands refers to what you want them to do or not do.

You may not get all of them as Supporters, but you need to get the majority of them, plus allies within the Resistors department actively working to bring about the change. Many will not sign on right away, but once your project demonstrates initial success, others will be willing to join your ranks. Everyone wants to be on the winning side.

Are there potential allies within the departments of your resisting stakeholders? People that will benefit from the success of your project?

Call to Action

Ask the following questions.

- *Which of your stakeholders have the most to gain as a result of your project?*
- *Which of your stakeholders have the most to lose?*

Refer back to your stakeholder analysis for both Resistors and Supporters.

How does the project help them? (Addresses pain or speaks to motivators)

Do you have enough senior representation from all of the affected groups that can address passive or active resistance to change within their teams?

Precondition 3: Develop a clear and compelling vision

If this is missing: Stakeholders and teams do not see or share the same vision of success. This leads to conflicts in project buy-in and in project execution. It becomes harder to recruit Supporters and harder to get the users to give the change a chance.

Remember

Where your stakeholder is in the organizational hierarchy directly correlates with their emphasis on vision. People executing in the operational division are focused on tasks and short-term results. Leaders at the strategic apex are focused only on the vision and strategy.

The vision is not about the technical or process change. Your vision is about how things will be better after the change. It describes how the change will help individuals and groups.

Your plan is not equal to your vision. The program is not equal to the vision. Your goals are not equal to the vision. Your vision is a clear, concise description that sets the stage for urgency of the change, describes the change only enough to describe how the future will look once the changes have been successful.

Vision guides decision making and aligns the plans and programs. The vision allows your project to correct course when it drifts. Your vision statement is an active tool. It does not get filed away or left to collect dust.

Your vision message needs to be tailored to your audience. Change may mean different things to different groups, and it usually does. What motivates one group may act as a deterrent for others.

Precondition 4: Constantly communicate the vision to everyone

If this is missing: Under-communicating the vision leads to project drift and ongoing disagreements about objectives, tasks, responsibilities and metrics.

You should be constantly sharing your vision, clarifying your vision and reinforcing your vision with your stakeholders throughout the project. When the teams are going through the difficult parts of the change, the vision helps remind them what the reward for their perseverance will be.

Reflect back to the vision with each plan development or change in project execution to ensure you aren't drifting away from your original vision. The project path will change from your original plan, but where you are going shouldn't.

Remember

Your project will always have obstacles or interruptions. Just like with physical navigation, if you don't get your bearings and re-align to your vision after an obstacle, you may have drifted so far that you can't get back on track.

Success will come from small, frequent, course corrections.

Communicating the vision is not just verbal. Words and actions need to align in communicating the vision or risk loss of credibility and increased resistance to change.

Precondition 5: Identify and remove obstacles

If this is missing: Obstacles, both real and perceived, block progress to realizing the new vision.

Change is difficult. It is painful. People struggle to implement change under ideal conditions. When people perceive their path to change to be blocked by obstacles, even small obstacles can stop them in their tracks.

The first step is to be able to identify the presence of those obstacles. This is where you need to be constantly out, working with the users and their managers to see the first signs of obstacles. Many of them are not physical obstacles, but obstacles of belief or perception. It could be existing job descriptions are written too narrowly and that prevents someone from shifting to take on new duties. It could be an old approval system or work-flow that does not permit team members to do the right thing at the right time according to the project requirements. In some cases, it may involve other systems like the bonus or incentive system that are now out of sync. The project expects a team member to focus on doing "B" while their bonus is based on their success at "A".

Remember

Incentives directly impact actions!

Organizational alignment, metrics and incentives is a larger topic. Imagine your sales organization is incented on, and focused on, new sales. Customer Service, however, is incented on customer satisfaction and service contract renewals. The result? Sales has an incentive to sell products or services into customer accounts even if Service can't keep the customer happy with what they've been sold.

The second step is to remove the obstacles. It may be as simple as re-training or coaching. It may involve re-writing job descriptions or developing new process flows. It may require re-aligning the organizational and reporting structure. This is one of the reasons that you need the powerful coalition described in Precondition 2.

Sometimes, removing obstacles requires you to address people who actively or passively block change. It may not be up to you personally as the project manager. It may not even be your primary stakeholder. That's another reason to build a large and powerful coalition that will contain enough business leaders to be able to address these Resistors in their own organization.

Have things suddenly slowed in an area of the project?

Are there areas where users are not adapting to the change?

If so, observe. Is it because they don't want to change or is it because there is an obstacle?
Who do you have in your coalition that can remove obstacles, whether it's people, process, structure or other systems?

If you don't have them, who do you need to recruit as a supporter?

Precondition 6: Design your project to deliver quick wins

If this is missing: Supporters and followers lose confidence in the project's chances of success. You lose credibility despite the hard work and progress. Perception shapes reality for your Supporters and Resistors.

Nobody has the energy or confidence to wait until the end of a multi-month or multi-year change project to see if they are going to be better off than before.

Your project needs to be designed to create short term and ongoing 'wins' that can be demonstrated and communicated. These wins re-motivate people and show that the change is worth the effort. These wins also encourage the undecided to join you as Supporters because everyone wants to be on the winning team.

The quick wins also demonstrate alignment between your words and your actions. You shared a vision of success and you delivered a part of it. This improves your credibility.

Your job as the project manager is to identify where these quick wins could happen and, if required, reconfigure the project execution to make these happen early and often. Don't start a project unless you can demonstrate successes quickly. If you wait for the one big win, you may be unpleasantly surprised when your project is shut down or placed under a new project manager.

What does a 'win' look like from any or all of your stakeholders' perspectives?

Are there any wins that can be achieved in the first two or three weeks of the project execution?

This could be a milestone deliverable, but ideally it would involve a concrete improvement to one of your user groups.

If that's not possible, use the milestone completion to refine the vision of success that you communicate. Show your stakeholders how the progress is tangible and will lead to more short-term wins.

Precondition 7: Finish the project

If this is missing: The project tapers off and eventually disappears from the consciousness of your organization. Every once in a while, users will ask "Whatever happened to project ABC?" The answer is that it died silently, like the organizational change projects before it. You and your organization lose credibility every time this happens and that makes it even more likely that your next project will fail. Your people have progressively fewer reasons to believe or to buy into your vision and are less willing to trust you when you ask them to undergo another change. You have lost credibility.

Remember

Credibility, like trust, can take a long time to build, but can be lost in a second.

This is the opposite of the previous problem. Celebrate the wins, but do not let the sense of urgency dissipate. 50% or 75% completion is not the same as project completion. Project success happens after all the work has been completed and final value has been delivered. After each quick win, you may need to re-evaluate, re-define and communicate the ongoing urgency to finish the project.

Your people need to see the quick wins as a sign that you can achieve success within the urgent situation that triggered the need for these changes. They can't rest on partial success as "good enough", and you can't let the sense of urgency diminish or they will stop there.

If the vision is no longer valid, then the project is over.

- If business conditions change
- If the project is no longer the direction your organization needs to go
- If the scope of change is outside what you can accomplish with a minor course correction or project change
  Then formally end the project.

Consider it a qualified success. Better yet, take the progress so far and use it as the first stage of the replacement project.

- Is the situation still urgent?
- If yes, how will you communicate that?
- If no, is the project complete or is there no further need for the project?

Precondition 8: Making the organizational change "the new normal"

If this is missing: Once the pressure of the change project is over, users will revert to the systems and processes they know and are familiar with. This will roll back any progress you made.

The project and the effort behind it do not actually end until the users are trained and comfortable in the new way of doing things such that they would not be more comfortable going back to the old way. This requires more than just including user training. It requires the project to have long enough timelines that allow the changes to stick before the project leadership moves on to their next project and stops verifying that the new processes are being followed. The old adage that new habits take 21 days to form has been disproven through studies (Lally & al, 2009). On average it can take 66 days for new habits to form, though the observed range was from 18 to 254 days based on the degree of challenge adopting the new habit. With that in mind, consider the following factors.

According to the users impacted by the change:

- Is the new system easier or harder to use?
- Are features that they used to use missing?
- Are they as efficient or more so on the new system than they were on the old system?
- Do not consider the project complete until the new system is second nature to the users and they can work at the same or better efficiency.

Sometimes You Need to Step Back or Bow Out

Depending on your organization and your own personality and motivations, the move to project leadership can be closely tied to your sense of self, to your work identity. Many of you will fight to get to lead your first few projects. When you assess your project to be a business transformation project, you need to assess your own skills and capabilities against the objectives to which you have been assigned.

While some of it may be ego driven, you will have to ask yourself whether delivering business value is more important than the prestige or recognition of leading the project.

When you are looking at business transformation, remember Precondition 2. It's easy to fail if you don't assemble the right people and empower them. This may mean bringing people with more power and authority to push the changes through. That may leave you more as a project administrator than leader. That may be the right thing to do.

The alternative is trying to maintain direct control and do it yourself. If the project itself fails with you firmly holding on to the wheel that results in a bad business outcome and a bad personal outcome.

Keys To Success

- Outside of your project, how aligned is IT with the Business?
- Within your project, are you able to align IT to the project vision in order to deliver customer or business value?
- How clear and concise is your vision statement? If you need more than twenty-four (24) words, you don't have a concise statement.
- Do your stakeholders have the same picture of success as you do when they hear you describe the vision?
- Do your stakeholders know how it relates to their pain points or motivators?
- Look at your additional stakeholders and the analysis you did (Transformation 5). Did you identify more than two Resistors? One Resistor and one or fewer Supporters? If so, you need to bring on more stakeholders (Supporters) as a part of the project guiding coalition.

Remember

Leading your communications with logical arguments will not achieve the results you need. There is no sense of urgency generated in a logical discussion. Urgency lives in the realm of emotion.

Pulling It All Together

Deconstruct your vision:

1. What is the problem you are trying to solve?

2. Why is it a problem?

3. What will happen if you don't do anything? What is the cost or impact?

4. What needs to change?

5. How will it change?

6. Who will the changes affect? (Positive and Negative)

7. Who will need to support those changes?

8. From their perspective, what value does the change bring them?

9. Go back to your stakeholder analysis. Does your answer above match at least one of their pain points or motivators? If not, go back and determine what's in it for them.

10. What will be different when the change is complete? (For those people or groups that underwent the change)

CHAPTER 7

CHECKPOINT AND
TROUBLESHOOTING

The six transformations covered in the previous chapters are not cosmetic changes. It's not a public relations campaign or a popularity contest. These are fundamental shifts in multiple areas, taking you outside of your comfort zone and into areas of growth.

Some of these will be easy for you and others will be challenging. The specifics will vary from person to person.

For those of you who find the transformations flowing naturally, you may find it valuable to review the material in three to six months to be able to fully realize the transformations.

Don't try to do too much or undertake too many transformations at the same time, or you won't be successful at any of them. Choose one, work on it until it becomes second nature, then move on to the next.

If, on the other hand, you find yourself stalled or stuck, the troubleshooting section below may help you get back on track.

132

Each of the sections below maps to one of the Six Transformations. If you are having difficulty in a particular Transformation, read the corresponding section. Since the Transformations are inter-related, consider reading the other sections as well to provide you even more insight.

Transformation 1: From Disillusioned to Eyes Wide Open

Why do I care?

You may not care. That's a value call you have to make for yourself. The tools and transformations presented here are valuable in a project context but that's not the only place they can be applied. If you don't see a need for these tools now (you're happy where you are, you don't want to reach out to non-technical stakeholders, you're satisfied with your project performance) then hold on to these tools, you may need them in the near future.

Why don't they try harder?

As the project manager or project leader, the success or failure starts and ends with you. Your stakeholder is your customer. The value that you provide to them is in delivering that project effectively. You can use the tools provided here to make it easier for your stakeholders and yourself to achieve success but, ultimately, it's your role to elicit the best from your stakeholders and your team.

Why is this my job?

See above. Your stakeholder benefits from a successful project but you are RESPONSIBLE for it. That's the nature of the PM/PL role.

I'm only responsible for technology.

There are three pieces of information you need to move forward.

- Who is the project manager?
- Is there a separate project for the Technical implementation and Business implementation?
- Do you have a written document that specifies that you are responsible only for the technical implementation?

If you're the project manager or the project leader, then you are not just responsible for technology. If there is a separate business project, then you are in the exact same place – you just have a different stakeholder and you are fully responsible to ensure all of the business value requirements are met for this business implementation project.

If you have a specific document that tells you that your scope is limited to the technology implementation only, then you're not the Project Manager or Project Leader. If those are your title and position, then you need to resolve the conflict in your authority and responsibility.

If you're not the Project Manager (and you know that) you can still use the tools and techniques provided to build your own capability and credibility. While you are doing that you can support your Project Manager and help them avoid the pitfalls you now know how to avoid.

Other pitfalls

- Bragging about how much you know about the business
- Talking outside of your scope of credibility (this changes as your credibility grows)
- Telling your stakeholders what they should be doing in their job or how they should be doing their jobs
- Don't fall in the 'If I was running the company we would…' trap.

Remember

Ask the following questions.

- *Who is your primary stakeholder?*
- *If you're not the project manager, who is? And, what's your role?*
- *Who are the customers that this project supports or impacts?*
- *What value does it provide them?*
- *What are the project success criteria?*

Transformation 2: From Tech Savvy to Business Savvy

We don't have customers.

You do have customers. You may not understand who they are yet. Your customer group may be much broader or narrower than you are currently thinking. Start by following the money. Where does your organization's money come from? See the tools at the end of this section to review.

I don't know who my external customers are.

This is common and normal. This is especially the case when you normally work in a department further away from where the customer value gets delivered. This is also common in public sector and not-for-profit organizations. It is closely tied with not understanding the value that your organization provides.

As above, where does the money come from? Direct from taxpayers? From donors? From the users of your goods and services? From customers that provide your goods or services to their own customers?

In many organizations the concept of an 'internal customer' is ever present. The use of a model like Porter's Value Chain can preserve the information your organization is trying to communicate while helping you focus on business and customer value.

We're government.

As government, public sector, or even Non-Governmental Organizations (NGO) you have customers and you add value.

Sometimes your customers are the taxpayers. Other times they are other governmental agencies.

The challenge with public sector analysis is simple. It is common to mistake the users of the service with your customers. They are often not the same and that seems to become more sharply defined as you move from local to regional and on to national levels of government.

On one end of the spectrum is when the customer is a direct service user. For example, when the taxpayers are your customers and they pay you directly, in property taxes, for curbside garbage pickup and disposal.

On the other extreme, capital infrastructure projects that are government funded. User of the infrastructure may be the road, bridge, or port user but the customer of an infrastructure project is the government. The value added is political currency. Governments in power value staying in power.

In a democracy, that translates to maintaining or increasing their share of the popular vote. In other forms of government, it can translate to reducing civil (unrest, unhappiness, dissatisfaction), minimizing the power of alternate or competing forms of government, and at the extreme, preventing uprisings or unwanted changes to the political structure.

How does my department add value?

While not project specific, sometimes your department is far enough away from your organization's customer that it can be hard to see where you fit in the value chain.
Start with a mind-map of your department, a simple one is included below. Fill in the actual departments and external entities your department interacts with.

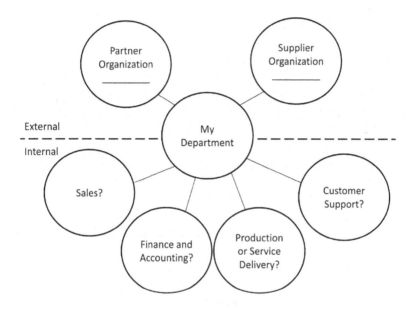

Figure 23: Value Chain Analysis with Mind Maps

Your next step is to identify which groups or departments provide inputs to your department (both internal and external), and then identify where the work that you do goes next. Normally there will be multiple streams, unless you have a very specialized department.

As an example, if your department has a help desk, you could analyze it by reviewing the inputs and outputs.

- Inputs may be end user calls, other support calls (internal technicians).
- Outputs might be break/fix, remote support or information/user assistance, knowledge base updates, product feedback to other technical teams for future consideration.

One value chain might look like:

- Helpdesk takes user or technician support calls that add value by remotely fixing or assisting in fixing a user problem
- Solving the user problem provides value by increasing the productivity of the business users (focus on the Primary functions)
- Increasing the productivity of users in the Primary functions provides increased Customer Value (or decreased cost of sales)

Another value chain might look like:

- Helpdesk take user or technician support calls and uses it to update the internal Knowledge Base (KB)
- End users can refer to the Knowledge Base to answer their own problems out of hours providing value through increasing user productivity without increasing the number of helpdesk staff required to cover phones 24 hours a day, providing business value (decreased cost of sales)
- Increasing the productivity of users in the primary functions provides increased customer value

You are enabling or enhancing the work of someone else who delivers customer value.

For more information on Porter's Primary and Secondary functions, see Chapter 8.

I don't know why we are doing this project?

If you know who your customers are, and you know what and where you add value for them but you're still not sure why this project exists, then consider the organization's strategy. Is this project expected to provide capabilities for a future initiative? Is the project a stop-gap or tactical measure until something supersedes it? Does it reduce the cost of goods (or services sold)?

There is one more possibility, and despite how we may feel, it is a rare one. Your project may not deliver business or customer value, but it may be designed to deliver personal or departmental value. It can be argued that this would allow that person or department to deliver future value more effectively, but that discussion is well outside the scope of this book.

If you have answered all of the above questions and you're still not sure, it's time to take that information and sit down with your stakeholder. Remember, you're asking in order to understand, to improve your ability to deliver project success.

Call to Action

Review your organization's and your department's website.

- *What does it tell you about your customers and value?*

Document your organizational and departmental mission and vision statements

- *Who contacts your organization?*
- *Who does your organization reach out to?*
- *Where does the money come from? Partnership? Taxation? Other departments? Charity?*
- *Where is the value? Is it a good or service? Good feelings? Political currency?*

Transformation 3: From Technical Resource to Strategic Partner

I know what I'm talking about but nobody listens to me.

Ask the following questions.

- Are you business savvy? Does what you talk about and focus on demonstrate that? (See Transformation 2)
- Do you have credibility in the job? (See Transformation 2)
- Do you have credibility with this stakeholder? (See Transformations 2, 3, 4 and 5)
- Do you have credibility that extends to this project? Is it close to what you're known for? (See Transformations 2 and 3)
- How is your department perceived in the organization? Is it the root of the problem, a service provider or a partner? (See Transformation 3)
- How much do you have an individual identity or reputation separate from your department, from the perspective of your stakeholders? (See Transformation 3)
- Are you adapting your communication to your Stakeholder's communication style(s)? (See Transformation 4)
- Do you conduct meetings with your stakeholders, Supporters and Resistors in 1:1 sessions, face to face, or do you rely on email and group meetings?

Call to Action

Use 1:1 meetings to get information, build credibility and tailor your message to your audience based on your analysis of their 3P.

They're not listening to me.

They are not listening to you because of two reasons.

- The message you're trying to deliver isn't connected with what the organization needs or wants in order to deliver business value.
- You have not delivered the change message in a way that is compatible with your stakeholders.

Review your stakeholder's communication style. Focus on what's in it for them (the business and your stakeholder). Tie the communications to what motivates each stakeholder. Make sure you deliver the message and address what matters to stakeholders (phrasing/delivery).

I told them it was going to happen, and it did!

Use the same approaches as laid out for the previous two challenges. Your issue is a combination of credibility, communication style and messaging (as it relates to what your stakeholders care about).

I'm a PM but I'm the only person on this project.

If you are the only person on the project, there are one of two probabilities.

- The project you're working on doesn't impact users in either what they do or how they do it. That makes it a procedure and not a project.
- The project you're working on has an impact on users and you need to expand the circle of people involved. Your stakeholder needs to understand how this project will impact others and where coordination, buy-in and sign-off need to come from. This should pave the way for increasing the scope and resourcing of your project.

I'm not comfortable changing how I dress. I don't want to change.

It's not changing, it's growing. You don't still wear what you wore to elementary school. Do you?

Remember

If you want to influence your organization, you need power. Positional Authority is your starting point, you won't succeed if you rely on that alone.

Building your power and credibility are inter-related. You won't be able to build power or credibility if you blend in with the rest of your department

---

Build personal power

- Information Power: Information you have or things you know
- Knowledge Power: What you know how to do
- Referent Power: The ability to influence those around you without use of direct authority

Build credibility

- Focus on what you've done in the past that relates to what you're doing now
- What's your track record for success?
- Use your portfolio of things that you've done
- Own your opinions, be upfront "I think ..." "Based on my experience..."
- Tie the objectives back to business and customer value, forget about the technology
- Call on the people who have had success in projects working with you

Break out of your IT/technical persona

Keep a log for the next ten days.

- How many hours a day do you spend at your desk?
- How much time do you spend in your stakeholders' departmental areas?
- How much time do you spend writing emails versus telephone calls versus face-to-face meetings?
  - Where do you spend your breaks and lunch?
  - At your desk?
  - With your technical colleagues?
  - With your stakeholders' teams?
- What percentage of your time is spent on leading your project versus other technical work?

Put yourself in your stakeholder's shoes and look at how you appear to them. Are you a partner in the project or do you blend into the IT background?

Transformation 4

My stakeholder doesn't listen to me.

There are several reasons your stakeholder may not be listening to you.

- Do you have credibility with them?
- Have you communicated in their preferred style?
- Have you translated the message to focus on what matters most to them?
- Did you summarize and deliver the level of detail they wanted?
- Were you able to deliver your message smoothly?

I don't know my stakeholder's communication style.

What do they talk about?

- Results and deliverables?
- Ideas?
- Process and steps?
- Personal stories?

How do they talk?

- Short, direct, focus on business?
- Explaining visions and ideas, jumping from point to point or subject to subject?
- Detailed, data driven, methodical and precise?
- Feelings and emotions?

If you don't know enough about your stakeholder, then talk to the people in your network, ideally your Supporters and listeners. Who has a good relationship with stakeholder?

I get flustered or draw a blank when I speak to my stakeholder.

There are typically two reasons that people get flustered: they don't know what they want to say, or they have trouble getting the words out easily.

To deal with the first, go through your stakeholder analysis. Make sure you know the 3Ps (Priorities, Perspectives and Personality) from Transformation 5 and then write out the message that you want to deliver. Make sure you account for your stakeholder's communication style and gear the message to what matters to your stakeholder.

To deal with the second, work on delivering your elevator pitch. Remember, the elevator pitch is not something you do to your stakeholder, it's a tool to get them to engage in a conversation about what matters to the two of you.

Remember

There are two parts to successful stakeholder communications. *Your message and why it matters to your stakeholder, and your delivery (is it easy for your stakeholder to get that message)*

To succeed:

- Determine your stakeholder's communications style
- Review your stakeholder analysis (3P) and review their priorities and perspectives
- Map out what you want to say before you say it
- Make sure that your talking points relate to your stakeholder's priorities and perspectives (and motivations)

Your elevator pitch is not designed to ambush your stakeholder, it's supposed to do three things:

1. Let the stakeholder know that what you want to talk about is important to them, not just to you. This leads to them asking you for more information.
2. Let the stakeholder assess how important and urgent this is for them. This leads to setting a time for you to meet formally and deliver the information that your stakeholder is interested in.
3. The stakeholder's responses and questions help you to prepare for your formal meeting. You know what's important, what they want to know more of, and how you have the solution to their problems.

Transformation 5

They keep changing their minds.

Ask the following questions.

- Review the vision. Is it crystal clear? Is there any ambiguity?
- Are the business requirements changing?
- Who is responsible for the business requirements?
- How well is success defined?

Everyone nods, but nobody does anything.

See Transformation 6.

Everyone nods, but then goes and does something different from what they agreed to.

Ask the following questions.

- Are the roles, responsibilities and deliverables clearly defined? Have they been agreed to?
- Do you have enough of the right Supporters?
- Do you have strong Resistors?
- Does your stakeholder see a problem?

See Transformation 6.

Users are now complaining because the system doesn't work the way they want it to, but we didn't have a choice.

For clarity of vision, see above. Ask the following questions.

- Is the success criteria well defined?
- Did the users have input?
- Did the users buy in?
- How was the project supposed to improve or deliver value?
- Who is supposed to sign off on behalf of the users? Were they a part of the project steering committee? Were they a supporter?

See Transformation 6.

Remember

Project success is defined. Project success is measured. You may have additional stakeholders that need to be analysed. You will need to gain or maintain their support based on their individual 3Ps.

Transformation 6

We kicked off a project and it went nowhere.

- Not enough urgency in the organization
- No agreement that there was a problem or what the problem was

No budget or resources.

- Low perceived business value or value poorly communicated
- Lack of credibility (either yours or your stakeholders)
- Too many Resistors and not enough Supporters

Everyone seemed to have a different idea on what the project was supposed to do.

- No agreement that there was a problem or what the problem was
- Too many Resistors and not enough Supporters
- Lack of shared (clear) vision

We started O.K. but then it stalled.

- Not enough urgency in the organization
- Lack of quick wins to re-motivate the people who had to carry the changes through

The next 'project of the month' came up and we moved on.

- Low business value, poor understanding of business value or organizational culture that does not prioritize business value
- Lack of actual senior executive sponsorship

Once they stopped forcing them, the users went back to doing things the old way.

- Failure to enforce or sustain the change (See Transformation 6)
- New systems did not support the users' actual work requirements
- Other organizational power factors at play
- Change in organizational requirements

Remember

Your vision is the key.

- *What is the problem that you are trying to solve?*
- *Why is it a problem?*
- *What is the impact of doing nothing?*
- *What needs to change to improve the situation?*

CHAPTER 8

TOOLS TO TAKE YOU TO THE NEXT LEVEL

This chapter presents a series of tools as reference, some that are covered in the Six Transformations, and some that are new and designed to extend your capability and effectiveness. They fall roughly into three categories.

- Freely available – references to help you dig deeper into a particular subject area
- Low cost – tools to help you solve specific problems or optimize certain activities. This includes good reference books.
- Other offerings – training courses, coaching and mentoring

You can go through this process using only free tools and information. There are plenty of good materials around! The difference is that with the free material, you need to determine your needs, curate and then digest the material. With the low-cost tools, some of that work is done for you. In the case of the paid offerings, the training and mentoring is tailored to you personally and provides two-way communications and feedback. The end result is that what you can accomplish in months with the free material, might only take weeks with the low-cost tools and days with intensive training.

The choice is yours.

Freely available tools and references

Due to the nature of freely available internet references, no URLs are provided below. Your search engine of choice will get you to where you need to go. Alternatively, you can check out www.tech2exceptional.com for a list of useful links and recommended reading.

S.W.O.T.

One of the simplest analysis techniques used for strategic planning. It stands for Strengths, Weaknesses, Opportunities and Threats. It can be a useful tool for brainstorming as well as for sharing the results of analysis with the wider team. The major pitfall with using SWOT for analysis stems from the acronym itself. To be used effectively you must reverse the order and analyze Opportunities and Threats first in order to have context for Strengths and Weaknesses.

Keywords online: SWOT analysis

Opportunities	Threats
Strengths	Weaknesses

Figure 24:SWOT Template

P.E.S.T.L.E.

Another mnemonic useful in strategic planning. It can be used to generate more targeted discussion and exploration because it explores more, and more defined dimensions. PESTLE stands for Political, Economic, Social, Technological, Legal and Environmental (some substitute E for Ethical). As a tool, the mnemonic remains flexible enough to scale down to analyze an individual market or scale up to accommodate national and international strategy.

Keywords online: PESTLE analysis, PEST analysis

Political
Economic
Social
Technological
Legal
Environmental

Table 3: PESTLE Template

Porter's Five Forces Model

Often used in conjunction with Porter's Generic Strategies.

Supplier Bargaining Power	Raw materials, components, labor, services and specialized knowledge
Buyer Bargaining Power	Readily available alternatives
Threat of Competitors	Economies of scale, brand loyalty, barriers to entry, perceived profitability
Threat of Substitutes	Ease of substitution, availability of substitutes, buyer switching costs and perceived levels of differentiation

Figure 25: Porter's Five Forces Overview

Competitive pressure is the combination of the previous four factors and tells you:

- How many direct competitors you have for a group of customers
- How your customers perceive your product or service
- How generic or differentiated it is from your competitors' products or services
- How much flexibility and control your organization has over product or service pricing
- Impact or value of pursuing Innovation strategies (increasing customer value) or optimization strategies (decreasing cost of delivering value)

From the perspective of understanding your organization's strategy, the threat of new competitors you most want to focus on is: Is there a customer need (value) that you are not fulfilling? That is most likely to align with your project and departmental objectives.
Keywords online: Porter Five Forces Model

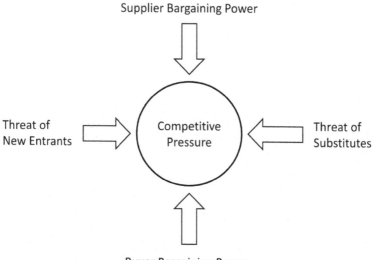

Figure 26: Four Forces Affecting Competitive Pressure

Porter's Generic Strategies

A matrix model used to explore and describe a choice of strategies available to firms based on the type of market environment (broadly focused versus narrowly focused or niche).

- Cost Leadership: Optimize the cost of goods or services so you can deliver them at market rates but achieve higher business value than competitors
- Cost (Focus): Segment your customer markets to create or target niches thereby reducing the number of competitors. Achieve cost leadership within those refined niches.
- Differentiation: Deliver new customer value by creating brand value and loyalty through the (customer) perceived differences in your product or service.
- Differentiation (Focus): Segment your customer markets to create or target niches thereby reducing the number of

competitors. Differentiate your product or service and create brand value and loyalty.

Keywords online: Porter Generic Strategies

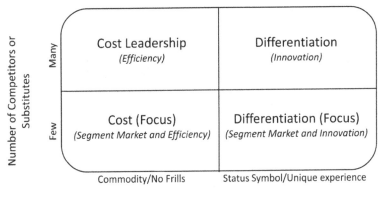

Figure 27: Porter's Generic Strategies (adapted)

Porter's Primary and Secondary Functions

In the value chain model, there are two types of organizational activities: Primary and secondary (or supporting) activities.

- Five primary activities deliver value directly to the customer
- Supporting activities encompass all the other activities that enhance, optimize and accelerate the primary activities.

It is important to understand the distinction because generating business value can happen in either Primary or Supporting Activities, by decreasing the cost of delivering value. Delivering increased customer value, by contrast, is only realized through innovation in the Primary activities.

Keywords online: Porter primary supporting functions

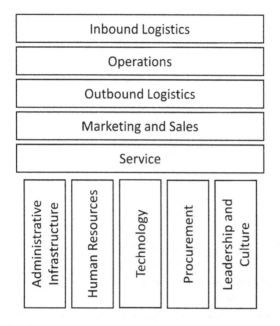

Figure 28: Porter's Primary and Supporting Activities (adapted)

Porter's Value Chain Analysis

The Value Chain can be used to demonstrate where and how groups, departments or projects add value to what will eventually be delivered as customer or business value. You need to understand where you fit in to value chain and how your project and the technology add value to the business.

Keywords online: Porter value chain

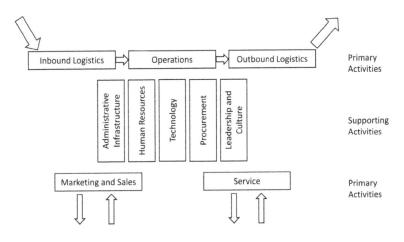

Figure 29: Porter's Value Chain Overview

Stakeholder Analysis Tools – 3P Model
Stakeholder Priorities:
- What is important to accomplish? To deliver?
- What do they want to avoid/minimize?
- Where do they spend their time? With whom and on what?
- What do they have on their whiteboard? What have they sent in email?
- What tasks do their people talk about or focus on?
- What is their department, position, role?
- What is someone in this role expected to do/deliver in the organization?

Stakeholder Perspectives:
- What words do they use?
- What are their hot buttons?
- What are their motivators?
- The perspectives of a Vice President of Sales will be very different from the Director of Customer Service and different again from the Chief Financial Officer

Stakeholder Personality:

- Communication style
- Are they more leaders (focused on effectiveness and change)?
- Are they more managers (focused on optimizing current processes and deliverables)?
- Their culture, educational experiences, work history

Resistor: _____

Priorities:

Perspectives:

Personality:

Table 4: Stakeholder Analysis: Resistor

Supporter: _____

Priorities:

Perspectives:

Personality:

Table 5: Stakeholder Analysis: Supporter

Stakeholder Satisfaction Matrix

The stakeholder satisfaction matrix is a visual reminder on how to effectively manage stakeholder interactions based on the degree of interest or participation a particular stakeholder has combined with their degree of influence on your project or activities.

Failure to meet the minimum requirement as described in the figure below will result in negative impact. Over-delivering in some of the quadrants effectively wastes time and energy you might have had for delivering higher quality results or improving engagement with your most important stakeholders.

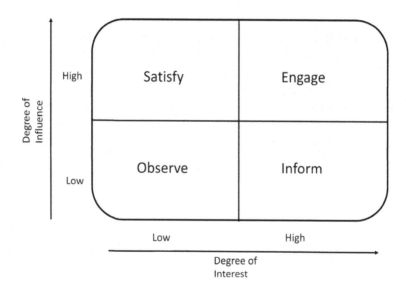

Figure 30: Stakeholder Satisfaction Priority

Low Cost Tools and References

While most of the items listed in this section are references, there are a few low-cost tools. They are not critical, but many readers may find them helpful.

Applications and online tools

Mind Mapping

Mind maps are visual representations of inter-related thoughts, ideas and concepts. They can be as simple or as complicated as you want them to be. They can be useful for a variety of activities, from group brainstorming to stakeholder and value chain analysis. While many people like the tactile aspects of pen and paper mind-maps, the electronic tools also have much to offer. You can look online for free mind mapping tools. What is available and what you get from the tools changes over time. Two reasonably enduring offerings include Xmind and Mindmaple.

HRDC Communications Style Assessment (Online)

HDRC offers an online Communications Style Assessment for individuals that can help you pinpoint your primary and secondary communication styles as well as offer ideas on how to flex to better interact with stakeholders who have other communication styles. Keywords: HRDC Communication Assessment

Visit www.tech2exceptional.com for other advanced offerings.

Books and other publications

Visit www.tech2exceptional.com for the most up-to-date list of books and other publications.

While most people will be able to realize the Transformations outlined in this book on their own, some of you may want or need a different approach of achieving those results

If you need additional assistance, please do not hesitate to send an e-mail at andrew@tech2exceptional.com, and I'd be more than happy to help. I came from the same technical background and it took me a while to transform my views from technical to exceptional. Don't be shy to reach out so that we can fast track your progress and get the most from your time and effort.

REFERENCES

Alessandra, A., & Hunsaker, P. (1993). *Communicating At Work.* New York: Simon & Schuster.

Bolton, R., & Bolton, G. (1984). *Social Style/Management Style.* New York: American Management Society.

Campbell, D. (1958). Common fate, similarity, and other indicies of the status of aggregates of persons as social entities. *Behavioural Sciences,* 14-25.

Delone, W., & McLean, E. (1992). Information Systems Success: The Quest for the Dependent Variable. *Information Systems Research.*

Delone, W., & McLean, E. (2002). Information Systems Success Revisited. *Proceedings of the 35th Hawaii International Conference on System Sciences.*

Hatzakis, T., & al, e. (2005). Towards the development of a social captial approach to evaluating change management interventions . *European Journal of Information Systems Vol 14, Issue 1.*

Honey, P., & Mumford, A. (1989). *Learning Styles Questionnaire.* King of Pussia: Organization Design & Development.

Kotter, J. (1996). *Leading Change.* Boston: Harvard Business Review Press.

Lally, P., & al, e. (2009). How are habits formed: Modelling habit formation in the real world. *European Journal of Social Psychology.*

Lucas, H. (1975). *Why Information systems fail.* Columbia University Press.

Merril, D., & Reid, M. (1981). *Personal Styles and Efective Performance: Make Your Personal Style Work for You.* Radnor: Chilton.

Mintzberg, H. (1973). *The nature of managerial work.* New York: Harper & Row.

Ranganath (Ratliff), K., & Nosek, B. (2008). Implicit attitude generalization occurs immediately, explicit attitude generalization takes time . *Psychological Science Issue 19.*

Reich, B., & Benbasat, I. (2000). Factors that influence the social dimension of alignment between business and information technology objectives. *MIS Quarterly Vol 24, No 1.*

Saur, C., Southon, G., & Dampney, C. (1997). Fit, Failure, and the House of Horrors: Towards a Configurational Theory of IS Project Failure. *ICIS 1997 Proceedings.*

Seddon, P., & al, e. (1999). Dimensions in Information Systems Success. *Communications of the Association for Information Systems: Volume 2, Article 20.*

Subrami, M., & al, e. (1999). Linking IS-User Partnerships to IS Performance: A Socio-Cognative Perspective. *MISRC Working Paper, University of Minnesota.*

INDEX

Made in the USA
Columbia, SC
08 April 2018